Alfred Wilks Drayson

Whist Laws and Whist Decisions

With upwards of 150 cases illustrating the laws: also remarks on the American laws

of whist and cases by which the reader's knowledge of the English laws may be

tested by himself

Alfred Wilks Drayson

Whist Laws and Whist Decisions
With upwards of 150 cases illustrating the laws: also remarks on the American laws of whist and cases by which the reader's knowledge of the English laws may be tested by himself

ISBN/EAN: 9783337248253

Printed in Europe, USA, Canada, Australia, Japan

Cover: Foto ©Suzi / pixelio.de

More available books at **www.hansebooks.com**

WHIST LAWS

AND

WHIST DECISIONS

WITH UPWARDS OF

150 CASES ILLUSTRATING THE LAWS

ALSO

REMARKS ON THE AMERICAN LAWS OF WHIST
AND CASES BY WHICH THE READER'S
KNOWLEDGE OF THE ENGLISH LAWS
MAY BE TESTED BY HIMSELF

BY

Major-Gen. A. W. DRAYSON
LATE R.A., F.R.A.S.

HON. MEMBER OF AMERICAN WHIST LEAGUE
AUTHOR OF "THE ART OF PRACTICAL WHIST"

NEW YORK
HARPER & BROTHERS PUBLISHERS
1896

CONTENTS

v

PREFACE

DURING a very long experience, I have found very few players who are thoroughly acquainted with the laws of whist. The majority of players have a superficial knowledge only; hence cases frequently occur where there is a dispute as to what (if any) penalty may be inflicted. When such disputes occur it is usual to refer to the laws; but it sometimes occupies a considerable time to find the law which refers to the special case. Even when the law is found, it is not unusual that something occurs to which the law does not exactly apply, or there is a margin given for doubt or difference of opinion. An excellent example of such a situation will be found in Case 93, and also in Cases 74 and 75.

In order to shorten as much as possible the time too frequently wasted in disputing, I have given a lengthy Index, referring to the laws and to the cases about which disputes have occurred, with the "decision" on each case.

These cases have accumulated during the past thirty years, and in nearly every instance have occurred scores of times in my own experience. To a person well acquainted with the laws and gifted with a legal mind, it may seem almost impossible that such disputes can occur, but they really do. Not long since I was a looker-on at a table where Z was a player. He had played whist for at least twenty-five years, and prided himself on his great knowledge of the game. His adversaries had revoked, but he had failed to detect this. A placed the cards for Z to cut. Z cut, and another bystander then said to Z, "Why did you not claim the revoke made by B?" "A revoke!" exclaimed Z. "Of course there was. I remember B trumped my heart, and played a heart on my last trick; but I will claim it now." "Too late," said B. "Not a bit; the deal is not completed," replied Z. A and B appealed to me. I quoted Law 78—that the cards having been cut, the penalty for the revoke could not be claimed. Z replied: "It is not the cut, it is the com-

pletion of the deal that prevents the revoke being claimed.   I will get the laws."
Z procured a copy of the laws, and commencing at Law 71, read slowly till he came
to 78, and then said, " Well, it's the first
time I knew that."

I could give scores of similar instances,
each showing how common it is for even
old players to remain many years ignorant
of the laws.   To prevent such mistakes, and
to enable players to readily refer when disputes do occur, this work has been written.

Reference has been made to the American laws, and in this book will be found a
means by which any reader may test his
knowledge of the laws of whist.

WHIST LAWS
AND WHIST DECISIONS

THE LAWS

1. The rubber is the best of three games. If the first two games be won by the same players, the third game is not played.

2. A game consists of five points. Each trick above six counts one point.

3. Honors, *i.e.*, ace, king, queen, and knave of trumps, are thus reckoned:

If a player and his partner, either separately or conjointly, hold—

    I. The four honors, they score four points.
    II. Any three honors, they score two points.
    III. Only two honors, they do not score.

4. Those players who, at the commencement of a deal, are at the score of four, cannot score honors.

5. The penalty for a revoke takes prece-

dence of all other scores. Tricks score next. Honors last.

6. Honors, unless claimed before the trump card of the following deal is turned up, cannot be scored.

7. To score honors is not sufficient; they must be called at the end of the hand; if so called, they may be scored at any time during the game.

8. The winners gain—

I. A treble, or game of three points, when their adversaries have not scored.

II. A double, or game of two points, when their adversaries have scored less than three.

III. A single, or game of one point, when their adversaries have scored three or four.

9. The winners of the rubber gain two points, commonly called the rubber points, in addition to the value of their games.

10. Should the rubber have consisted of three games, the value of the loser's game is deducted from the gross number of points gained by their opponents.

11. If an erroneous score be proved, such mistake can be corrected prior to the conclusion of the game in which it occurred, and such game is not concluded until the

trump card of the following deal has been turned up.

12. If an erroneous score affecting the amount of the rubber be proved, such mistake can be rectified at any time during the rubber.

CUTTING

13. The ace is the lowest card.

14. In all cases, every one must cut from the same pack.

15. Should a player expose more than one card, he must cut again.

FORMATION OF TABLE

16. If there are more than four candidates, the players are selected by cutting: those first in the room having the preference. The four who cut the lowest cards play first, and again cut to decide on partners; the two lowest play against the two highest; the lowest is the dealer, who has choice of cards and seats, and having once made his selection must abide by it.

17. When there are more than six candidates, those who cut the two next lowest cards belong to the table, which is complete

with six players; on the retirement of one
of these six players the candidate who cut
the next lowest card has a prior right to any
after-comer to enter the table.

CUTTING CARDS OF EQUAL VALUE

18. Two players cutting cards of equal
value, unless such cards are the two highest, cut again; should they be the two lowest, a fresh cut is necessary to decide which
of the two deals.

19. Three players cutting cards of equal
value cut again. Should the fourth (or remaining) card be the highest, the two lowest of the new cut are partners, the lower
of these two the dealer; should the fourth
card be the lowest, the two highest are partners, the original lowest the dealer.

CUTTING OUT

20. At the end of a rubber, should admission be claimed by any one or two candidates, he who has, or they who have,
played a greater number of consecutive rubbers than the others is, or are, out; but
when all have played the same number,

they must cut to decide upon the out-goers; the highest are out.

ENTRY AND RE-ENTRY

21. A candidate wishing to enter a table must declare such intention prior to any of the players having cut a card, either for the purpose of commencing a fresh rubber or of cutting out.

22. In the formation of fresh tables, those candidates who have neither belonged to nor played at any other table have the prior right of entry; the others decide their right of admission by cutting.

23. Any one quitting a table prior to the conclusion of a rubber may, with consent of the other three players, appoint a substitute in his absence during that rubber.

24. A player cutting into one table, while belonging to another, loses his right of re-entry into that latter, and takes his chance of cutting in, as if he were a fresh candidate.

25. If any one break up a table, the remaining players have the prior right to him of entry into any other; and should there not be sufficient vacancies at such other ta-

ble to admit all these candidates, they set-
tle their precedence by cutting.

SHUFFLING

26. The pack must neither be shuffled
below the table, nor so that the face of any
card be seen.

27. The pack must not be shuffled during
the play of the hand.

28. A pack, having been played with,
must neither be shuffled by dealing it into
packets nor across the table.

29. Each player has a right to shuffle,
once only, except as provided by Rule 32,
prior to a deal, after a false cut, or when a
new deal has occurred.

30. The dealer's partner must collect the
cards for the ensuing deal, and has the first
right to shuffle that pack.

31. Each player, after shuffling, must place
the cards, properly collected and face downwards, to the left of the player about to deal.

32. The dealer has always the right to
shuffle last; but should a card or cards be
seen during his shuffling, or while giving
the pack to be cut, he may be compelled to
reshuffle.

THE DEAL

33. Each player deals in his turn; the right of dealing goes to the left.

34. The player on the dealer's right cuts the pack, and in dividing it must not leave fewer than four cards in either packet; if in cutting, or in replacing one of the two packets on the other a card be exposed, or if there be any confusion of the cards, or a doubt as to the exact place in which the pack was divided, there must be a fresh cut.

35. When a player whose duty it is to cut has once separated the pack, he cannot alter his intention; he can neither reshuffle nor recut the cards.

36. When the pack is cut, should the dealer shuffle the cards he loses his deal.

A NEW DEAL

37. There must be a new deal—

I. If during a deal, or during the play of a hand, the pack be proved incorrect or imperfect.

II. If any card, excepting the last, be faced in the pack.

38. If while dealing a card be exposed by the dealer or his partner, should neither of the adversaries have touched the cards, the latter can claim a new deal; a card exposed by either adversary gives that claim to the dealer, provided that his partner has not touched a card; if a new deal does not take place the exposed card cannot be called.

39. If during dealing a player touch any of his cards, the adversaries may do the same without losing their privilege of claiming a new deal, should chance give them such option.

40. If in dealing one of the last cards be exposed, and the dealer turn up the trump before there is reasonable time for his adversaries to decide as to a fresh deal, they do not thereby lose their privilege.

41. If a player, while dealing, look at the trump card, his adversaries have a right to see it, and may exact a new deal.

42. If a player take into the hand dealt to him a card belonging to the other pack, the adversaries, on discovery of the error, may decide whether they will have a fresh deal or not.

A MISDEAL

43. A misdeal loses the deal.

44. It is a misdeal—

I. Unless the cards are dealt into four packets, one at a time in regular rotation, beginning with the player to the dealer's left.

II. Should the dealer place the last card (*i.e.,* the trump) face downwards, on his own, or any other pack.

III. Should the trump card not come in its regular order to the dealer ; but he does not lose his deal if the pack be proved imperfect.

IV. Should a player have fourteen cards, and either of the other three less than thirteen.

V. Should the dealer, under an impression that he has made a mistake, either count the cards on the table or the remainder of the pack.

VI. Should the dealer deal two cards at once, or two cards to the same hand, and then deal a third ; but if prior to dealing that third card the dealer can, by altering the position of one card only, rectify such error, he may do so, except as provided by the second paragraph of this law.

VII. Should the dealer omit to have the pack cut to him, and the adversaries discover the error, prior to the trump card being turned up, and before looking at their cards, but not after having done so.

45. A misdeal does not lose the deal if, during the dealing, either of the adversaries touch the cards prior to the dealer's partner having done so; but should the latter have first interfered with the cards, notwithstanding either or both of the adversaries have subsequently done the same, the deal is lost.

46. Should three players have their right number of cards, the fourth have less than thirteen, and not discover such deficiency until he has played any of his cards, the deal stands good; should he have played, he is as answerable for any revoke he may have made as if the missing card, or cards, had been in his hand; he may search the other pack for it, or them.

47. If a pack, during or after a rubber, be proved incorrect or imperfect, such proof does not alter any past score, game, or rubber; that hand in which the imperfection was detected is null and void; the dealer deals again.

48. Any one dealing out of turn, or with the adversary's cards, may be stopped before the trump card is turned up, after which the game must proceed as if no mistake had been made.

49. A player can neither shuffle, cut, nor deal for his partner without the permission of his opponents.

50. If the adversaries interrupt a dealer while dealing, either by questioning the score or asserting that it is not his deal, and fail to establish such claim, should a misdeal occur he may deal again.

51. Should a player take his partner's deal, and misdeal, the latter is liable to the usual penalty, and the adversary next in rotation to the player who ought to have dealt then plays.

THE TRUMP CARD

52. The dealer, when it is his turn to play to the first trick, should take the trump card into his hand ; if left on the table after the first trick be turned and quitted, it is liable to be called ; his partner may at any time remind him of the liability.

53. After the dealer has taken the trump card into his hand it cannot be asked for ; a player naming it at any time during the play of that hand is liable to have his highest or lowest trump called.

54. If the dealer take the trump card into his hand before it is his turn to play he may

be desired to lay it on the table ; should he show a wrong card, this card may be called, as also a second, a third, etc., until the trump card be produced.

55. If the dealer declare himself unable to recollect the trump card, his highest or lowest trump may be called at any time during that hand, and, unless it cause him to revoke, must be played ; the call may be repeated, but not changed, *i. e.*, from highest to lowest, or *vice versa*, until such card is played.

CARDS LIABLE TO BE CALLED

56. All exposed cards are liable to be called, and must be left on the table ; but a card is not an exposed card when dropped on the floor, or elsewhere below the table.

The following are exposed cards :

I. Two or more cards played at once.

II. Any card dropped with its face upwards, or in any way exposed on or above the table, even though snatched up so quickly that no one can name it.

57. If any one play to an imperfect trick the best card on the table, or lead one which is a winning card as against his ad-

versaries, and then lead again, or play several such winning cards, one after the other, without waiting for his partner to play, the latter may be called on to win, if he can, the first or any other of those tricks, and the other cards thus improperly played are exposed cards.

58. If a player, or players, under the impression that the game is lost, or won, or for other reasons, throw his or their cards on the table face upwards, such cards are exposed, and liable to be called, each player's by the adversary ; but should one player alone retain his hand, he cannot be forced to abandon it.

59. If all four players throw their cards on the table face upwards, the hands are abandoned ; and no one can again take up their cards. Should this general exhibition show that the game might have been saved, or won, neither claim can be entertained, unless a revoke be established. The revoking players are then liable to the following penalties : they cannot, under any circumstances, win the game by the result of that hand, and the adversaries may add three to their score, or deduct three from that of the revoking players.

60. A card detached from the rest of the hand so as to be named is liable to be called; but should the adversary name a wrong card, he is liable to have a suit called when he or his partner have the lead.

61. If a player, who has rendered himself liable to have the highest or lowest of a suit called, fail to play as desired, or if when called on to lead one suit lead another, having in his hand one or more cards of that suit demanded, he incurs the penalty of a revoke.

62. If any player lead out of turn, his adversaries may either call the card erroneously led, or may call a suit from him or his partner when it is the next turn of either of them to lead.

63. If any player lead out of turn, and the other three have followed him, the trick is complete, and the error is rectified; but if only the second, or the second and third, have played to the false lead, their cards, on discovery of the mistake, are taken back. There is no penalty against any one excepting the original offender, whose card may be called, or he, or his partner, when either of them has next the lead, may be compelled to play any suit demanded by the adversaries.

64. In no case can a player be compelled to play a card which would oblige him to revoke.

65. The call of a card may be repeated until such card has been played.

66. If a player called on to lead a suit have none of it, the penalty is paid.

CARDS PLAYED IN ERROR, OR NOT PLAYED TO A TRICK

67. If the third hand play before the second, the fourth hand may play before his partner.

68. Should the third hand not have played, and the fourth play before his partner, the latter may be called on to win or not to win the trick.

69. If any one omit playing to a former trick, and such error be not discovered until he has played to the next, the adversaries may claim a new deal. Should they decide that the deal stand good, the surplus card at the end of the hand is considered to have been played to the imperfect trick, but does not constitute a revoke.

70. If any one play two cards to the same trick, or mix his trump or other card with

2

a trick to which it does not properly belong, and the mistake be not discovered
until the hand is played out, he is answerable for all consequent revokes he may have
made. If during the play of the hand the
error be detected, the tricks may be counted face downwards, in order to ascertain
whether there be among them a card too
many. Should this be the case, they may
be searched and the card restored. The
player is, however, liable for all revokes he
may meanwhile have made.

THE REVOKE

71. Is when a player, holding one or more
cards of the suit led, plays a card of a different suit.

72. The penalty for a revoke:

I. Is at the option of the adversaries, who, at
the end of the hand, may either take three tricks
from the revoking player, or deduct three points
from his score, or add three to their own score ;

II. Can be claimed for as many revokes as occur during the hand ;

III. Is applicable only to the score of the game
in which it occurs ;

IV. Cannot be divided, *i. e.*, a player cannot

add one or two to his own score and deduct one or two from the revoking player ;

V. Takes precedence of every other score, *e. g.*, the claimants two, their opponents nothing ; the former add three to their score, and thereby win a treble game, even should the latter have made thirteen tricks, and held four honors.

73. A revoke is established, if the trick .in which it occur be turned and quitted, *i. e.*, the hand removed from that trick after it has been turned face downwards on the table ; or if either the revoking player or his partner, whether in his right turn or otherwise, lead or play to the following trick.

74. A player may ask his partner whether he has not a card of the suit which he has renounced ; should the question be asked before the trick is turned and quitted, subsequent turning and quitting does not establish the revoke, and the error may be corrected, unless the question be answered in the negative, or unless the revoking player or his partner have led or played to the following trick.

75. At the end of the hand the claimants of a revoke may search all the tricks.

76. If a player discover his mistake in

time to save a revoke, his adversaries, whenever they think fit, may call the card thus played in error, or may require him to play his highest or lowest card to that trick in which he has renounced ; any player or players who have played after him may withdraw their cards and substitute others; the cards withdrawn are not liable to be called.

77. If a revoke be claimed, and the accused player or his partner mix his cards before they have been sufficiently examined by the adversaries, the revoke is established. The mixing of the cards only renders the proof of a revoke difficult, but does not prevent the claim, and possible establishment, of the penalty.

78. A revoke cannot be claimed after the cards have been cut for the following deal.

79. The revoking player and his partner may, under all circumstances, require the hand in which the revoke had been detected to be played out.

80. If a revoke occur, be claimed, and proved, bets on the odd trick, or on amount of score, must be decided by the actual state of the latter after the penalty is paid.

81. Should the players on both sides sub-

ject themselves to the penalty of one or more revokes, neither can win the game; each is punished at the discretion of his adversary.

82. In whatever way the penalty be enforced, under no circumstances can a player win a game by the result of the hand during which he has revoked; he cannot score more than four.

CALLING FOR NEW CARDS

83. Any player (on paying for them) before, but not after, the pack be cut for the deal, may call for fresh cards. He must call for two new packs, of which the dealer takes his choice.

GENERAL RULES

84. Where a player and his partner have an option of exacting from their adversaries one of two penalties, they should agree who is to make the election, but must not consult with one another which of the two penalties it is advisable to exact; if they do so consult, they lose their right; and if either of them, with or without consent of his partner, demand a penalty to which *he is*

entitled, such decision is final. This rule does
not apply in exacting the penalties for a revoke, partners *have then a right to consult.*

85. Any one during the play of a trick, or
after the four cards are played, and before,
but not after, they are touched for the purpose of gathering them together, may demand that the cards be placed before their
respective players.

86. If any one, prior to his partner playing, should call attention to the trick, either
by saying that it is his, or by naming his
card, or, without being required so to do, by
drawing it towards him, the adversaries may
require that opponent's partner to play the
highest or lowest of the suit they led, or to
win or lose the trick.

87. In all cases where a penalty has been
incurred, the offender is bound to give reasonable time for the decision of his adversaries.

88. If a bystander make any remark which
calls the attention of a player or players to
an oversight affecting the score, he is liable
to be called on, by the players only, to pay the
stakes and all bets on that game or rubber.

89. A bystander, by agreement among the
players, may decide any question.

90. A card or cards torn or marked must be either replaced by agreement, or new cards called at the expense of the table.

91. Any player may demand to see the last trick turned, and no more. Under no circumstances can more than eight cards be seen during the play of the hand, viz., the four cards on the table which have not been turned and quitted, and the last trick turned.

ETIQUETTE OF WHIST

The following rules belong to the established Etiquette of Whist. They are not called laws, as it is difficult—in some cases impossible — to apply any penalty to their infraction, and the only remedy is to cease to play with players who habitually disregard them :

I. Two packs of cards are invariably used at clubs ; if possible, this should be adhered to.

II. Any one, having the lead and several winning cards to play, should not draw a second card out of his hand until his partner has played to the first trick, such act being a distinct intimation that the former has played a winning card.

III. No intimation whatever, by word or gesture, should be given by a player as to the state of his hand or of the game.

IV. A player who desires the cards to be placed, or who demands to see the last trick, should do it for his own information only, and not in order to invite the attention of his partner.

V. No player should object to refer to a bystander who professes himself uninterested in the game, and able to decide any disputed question of facts — as to who played any particular card, whether honors were claimed, though not scored, or *vice versa*, etc. It is unfair to revoke purposely. Having made a revoke, a player is not justified in making a second in order to conceal the first.

VI. Until the players have made such bets as they wish, bets should not be made with bystanders.

VII. Bystanders should make no remarks, neither should they by word or gesture give any intimation of the state of the game until concluded and scored, nor should they walk round the table to look at the different hands.

VIII. No one should look over the hand of a player against whom he is betting.

DUMMY

Is played by three players.

One hand, called dummy's, lies exposed on the table.

The laws are the same as those of whist, with the following exceptions:

I. Dummy deals at the commencement of each rubber.

II. Dummy is not liable to the penalty for a revoke, as his adversaries see his cards; should he revoke and the error not be discovered until the trick is turned and quitted, it stands good.

III. Dummy being blind and deaf, his partner is not liable to any penalty for an error whence he can gain no advantage. Thus he may expose some or all of his cards, or may declare he has the game or trick, etc., without incurring any penalty; if, however, he lead from dummy's hand when he should lead from his own, or *vice versa*, a suit may be called from the hand which ought to have led.

DOUBLE DUMMY

Is played by two players, each having a dummy or exposed hand for his partner. The laws of the game do not differ from Dummy Whist, except in the following special law: There is no misdeal, as the deal is a disadvantage.

AMERICAN WHIST LAWS

(*As revised and adopted at the Third American Whist Congress,* 1893.)

WHIST has taken a great hold in America. An excellent paper termed *Whist* is published monthly, while the American Whist League includes numerous clubs in all parts of the United States.

While the English " Laws of Whist " are comprised under ninety-one headings, the Americans have condensed these under thirty-nine headings.

The general principles of the game are the same in America as in England, so that a good player in England might visit America and join a rubber there without finding that he was playing a game unknown to him.

The laws in both countries are almost identical; the few differences made by the Americans are, in my opinion, in nearly every case improvements. These differences will now be referred to.

In the American Whist Laws no mention is made of counting honors. The game consists of seven points, instead of five. The value of the game is determined by deducting the loser's score from seven.

These two alterations tend to diminish the effect of what is termed "luck," and hence to increase the value of play. This is undoubtedly an improvement in a game of skill.

It has always seemed to me that by our English laws honors count too much, and thus chance, or luck, has too much influence on the result of the game. My partner and I may be at the score of three, and the adversaries also at the score of three; by careful play I may win the odd trick; but the adversaries hold two by honors and score game, and the odd trick, which I won, is not of the slightest advantage to me.

Again, when the score is love all, I hold four by honors, but lose the trick; the score is therefore four to me, one to the adversaries. In the next hand the adversaries hold four by honors, but I win the trick; and as tricks count before honors, I win a double on that game, though I and the adversaries held similar cards. Had the order of the

cards been reversed, and the adversaries
had first held the four by honors, then they
would have won a double on the game.
These chances necessarily reduce the value
of good sound play, and tend to make whist
more a game of chance than of skill.

It has been urged that if whist became
more a game of skill, and less of chance,
bad or indifferent players would not join
in it as freely as they now do. I reply, so
much the better; there is nothing so trying
to the patience and temper as when there
are three good players and one very bad.
This bad player spoils the rubber, and entirely upsets all the calculations of the good
players; and as there seems to be compen-
sation in some games of chance, the bad
player usually holds very good cards, and
necessarily wins. He then boasts that in
spite of his adversaries being supposed first-
class players, yet he won the rubber against
them, so that he must be more skilful than
they are.

Eliminating honors and making the game
seven instead of five are, I consider, great
improvements in whist. Under the head
of " Misdeal," Law 44, Section, 5, English
code, it is stated : " Should the dealer, un-

der an impression that he has made a mistake, either count the cards on the table or remainder of the pack," it is a misdeal. The wording of this law is bad : a quibbler may stop during the deal and begin to count the cards; the adversaries would claim a misdeal.

"Certainly not," would say the quibbler. "There is nothing in the laws against my counting the cards. I am not under the impression that I have made a misdeal; I know I have not done so. I may count the cards if I choose."

By Rule 17, Section 3, of the American code, it says: It is a misdeal "if he counts the cards on the table or in the remainder of the pack." No mention being made as to the "impression" of the dealer. By the English code, if the trump card be left on the table after the first trick is turned and quitted, it is liable to be called. By the American code, if the trump card be left on the table after the *second* trick is turned and quitted, it is liable to be called (Law 18). This is an unimportant difference.

Under the heading "Irregularities in the hand," the Americans have made an important difference in the law. By Law 44,

Section 4, English code: "Should a player have fourteen cards and either of the other three less than thirteen," it is a misdeal.

In the first edition of *The Art of Practical Whist* I called attention to the defect or obscurity of this law. By the American code an attempt is made to remedy this defect, but it does not seem to me that the difficulty is entirely avoided.

Rule 19 of the American code is as follows: "If at any time after all have played to the first trick, the pack being perfect, a player is found to have either more or less than his correct number of cards, and his adversaries have their right number, the latter, upon the discovery of such surplus or deficiency, may consult and shall have the choice—

"I. To have a new deal ; or,

"II. To have the hand played out, in which case the surplus or missing card, or cards, are not taken into account.

"III. If either of the adversaries also has more or less than his correct number there must be a new deal."

This law is certainly a far better one than our English law, as it prevents the careless

players who play with fourteen and twelve
cards from scoring anything if a new deal
is demanded. If, however, the non-offending players elect to have the hand played
out, they may have overrated their strength,
and may lose two or three on the hand.
That which I suggested in Case 19, *The
Art of Practical Whist*, seems to me to
more fully meet the case: "If two partners
hold twenty-six cards between them, one
holding more, the other less than thirteen,
while the adversaries hold thirteen each, no
score made by the partners holding the un-
equal number of cards can be counted in that
hand, whereas any score made by the partners holding thirteen each can be counted."

As regards "cards liable to be called,"
the American laws differ from the English.
By the English code you may lower the
whole of your hand so that your partner
may see nearly every card in it, but there is
no penalty for doing so. In Case 29, *The
Art of Practical Whist*, I called attention
to the defect in this law. By the American
code an attempt is made to remedy this
defect. Law 20, Section 3, states: "Every
card so held by a player that his partner
sees any portion of its face." Section 4:

" All the cards in a hand lowered or shown by a player so that his partner sees more than one card of it."

Who is to be the judge as to whether the cards were sufficiently lowered to enable the partner to see them? One partner might sit very tall, another very short, the angle at which the cards were lowered might enable the tall partner to see them, while the same angle of lowering would not enable the short partner to do so. Who is to judge of the angle? It would be merely a matter of opinion on the part of the adversaries, and when a question comes to a matter of opinion it must end in an unsatisfactory dispute.

Again, by the English code, if two cards are played together or led together, either may be called, and the card not called is an exposed card. By the American code, " Every card thrown with the one led or played to the current trick " (is an exposed card). " The player must indicate the one led or played."

Suppose I hold ace, queen of a suit, and am last player; third hand plays king; I throw ace and queen on the table at the same time. I indicate that I play the ace, and

then lead the queen. By the American code
I scarcely suffer for this carelessness; by the
English code, my queen can be called on
the king. I do not think this American law
is good, as it gives so many chances for a
careless player to escape from any penalty.

LEADING OUT OF TURN

By the English code the card led in error
may be called, or a suit can be called by
either adversary when it is the turn of the
offending player or his partner next to
lead. By the American code, Law 24: " If
any player leads out of turn, a suit may be
called from him or his partner the first time
it is the turn of either of them to lead. The
penalty can be enforced only by the adversary on the right of the player from
whom a suit can be lawfully called."

Thus, by the English code, two penalties
may be enforced, viz., calling the card or calling a lead, and either adversary may elect
to enact this penalty. By the American
code a lead only can be called, and only one
adversary can enact the penalty. This is
certainly a reduction of the punishment for
careless play.

THE REVOKE

By the English code either of three penalties may be enacted for a revoke, viz.: the non - revoking players may add three to their score, they may deduct three from the score of the revoking players, or they may take three tricks from the revoking players and add them to their own.

By the American code, Law 30, there is only one penalty, viz., the "transfer of two tricks from the revoking side to their adversaries." This again is a considerable reduction of the penalty, and in more than one instance may be no penalty at all.

For example, suppose both sides are at the score of four. One side wins three by cards, hence win game, the value of the game being three; but it is found the other side has revoked. The revoking side in no way suffer for this revoke, as the adding of two tricks makes no difference. This would also hold good if the revoking players were at any other score, and the non-revoking players won game without the aid of the penalty for the revoke. Considering how frequently a revoke fails to be discovered, I think the penalty should be very severe.

By the English code, if a player say, " I have game in my hand, I can win the rest," there is no penalty. By the American code, Law 36, the partner's cards must be laid upon the table, and are liable to be called.

In the first edition of *The Art of Practical Whist"* I referred to the great annoyance caused by unobservant players who were perpetually wanting to look at the last trick, and I regretted that Law 91, English code, existed. The first club that put a penalty on looking at the last trick was, I believe, a whist club at Melbourne, Australia. Any player asking to look at the last trick was fined sixpence. By the American code, Law 37, " When a trick has been turned and quitted, it must not again be seen until after the hand has been played. A violation of this law subjects the offender's side to the same penalty as in case of a lead out of turn."

This law is a great improvement on Law 91, English code, and it is to be hoped that means may be found for adopting the American law in the English game.

At the end of Law 39, American code, " If the wrong adversary demands a penalty, or a wrong penalty is demanded, none can be enforced."

The above is an unwritten law of the English code as far as the wrong penalty. With the above exceptions, American and English whist is the same. The " Etiquette of Whist " by the American code differs, as far as I can see, in no respect from the English; they are both framed to repress improprieties of conduct not reached by the laws, and for which no penalties could well be enforced.

There is, however, one very common breach, perhaps more of good manners than of etiquette, from which I have frequently suffered. I am not a smoker, but when I have joined a rubber a looker-on would sit on each side of me and smoke pipes, while another stood behind me, all puffing their smoke over me. I have frequently had to cease playing in consequence of this annoyance, as one does not like to complain repeatedly of such proceedings.

Pages might be written on the breaches of etiquette committed by persons who join a rubber of whist, and who consequently tend to prevent this rubber from being the intellectual and social enjoyment that it ought to be. In *The Field*, March 30 and April 6, 1889, I wrote two articles on " The

Etiquette of Whist." Unfortunately, those
who commit the most serious breaches of
etiquette seem to be those who never read
and never learn ; as I have found, even quite
recently, many persons who invariably commit day after day those very breaches of
etiquette to which I directed attention in
those articles.

In the second of these articles is the
following sentence : " There is no greater
breach of etiquette than for an adversary to
attempt to claim a penalty to which he is
not entitled. Such a proceeding must be
assumed to be due to ignorance only. The
penalty for such an incorrect claim is now
very justly decided to be that the original
offender is released from all punishment for
his offence. To play a game during many
years without making one's self acquainted
with the laws which govern this game is
not an unusual proceeding."

As a guide to individuals, as a reference
for clubs and all whist-players, I believe the
cases given in this small work will be found
of use. The index will greatly help to quickly find those cases about which disputes may
occur. To experienced whist-players many
of these disputed cases may appear almost

childish, but they have occurred scores of times in my own experience.

DISPUTES ABOUT PENALTIES

When disputes occur relative to penalties for offences committed against the laws of whist, these usually come under three heads, viz.:

I. Ignorance of the laws.

II. Misreading or forgetting the law suitable to deal with the offence.

III. Incompetency for reasoning soundly on the application of the law.

When such disputes occur it is desirable to be able, without delay or unnecessary search, to refer to the law which bears on the dispute, or to cases which come so very close to the question at issue that there can be little or no doubt what the law really is. To meet this desideratum I have endeavored, by an extensive index, to enable the rule, or law, and special cases to be readily found. It seems quite impossible to frame laws for every special case, as some players practise such eccentric proceedings that no reasonable person would ever even dream that such acts could be committed, yet they are; then the law most nearly bearing on the special case may be applicable. In spite of all the laws and the cases, there may yet occur offences which present difficulties as regards the penalty to be enacted; these cases are, however, now rare, as whist legislation is certainly in an advanced condition.

In the index I have adopted the alphabetical code as that most suitable for reference. When a case occurs about which there is a dispute, and none of the laws or the decisions seem to bear exactly on the case, a statement of the facts should be drawn out, and the contending parties must agree that the facts are correctly stated. This document should be at once posted to the selected referee, such, for example, as *The Field*, and the decision of *The Field* should be binding.

It has happened, and may happen again, that both the disputing parties are more eager to prove they are right in their opinions than that a just decision should be given, and a very slight alteration in the wording of the case may make all the difference in the referee's decision. I know a case where a dispute occurred between A and Y relative to a penalty. A drew out a statement of facts, and read this to Y, B, and Z. B and Z agreed that the statement was correct. Y said, "Yes, very nearly correct; let me have the statement." A handed the statement to Y under the belief that Y would alter anything to which he did not agree, and again submit it to A. The next day Y announced that he had posted the case to the referee, and in due course the referee's decision was received, and, much to the surprise of B, Z, and A, it was in Y's favor.

It was weeks after this that A discovered that before posting the statement Y had altered two words, which quite changed the case. Hence such precautions about posting, etc., as I have mentioned, are by no means unnecessary.

The very slightest difference in the facts, or words used, may make all the difference in the decision. For example, A says, "Shall we call a suit?" This is a consultation, and A loses his right to claim a penalty. If, however, A claims that the words he used were, " I shall call a suit," this is not a consultation, but an announcement of the pen-

alty he intended to inflict. Where possible
the case should be written on a large sheet
of paper, and the decision written under it,
so that the question and answer may both
be before the reader.

When questions are referred to *The Field*
a copy of the question should be retained
by the sender, and the decision should be
gummed under the question.

On looking over the replies in *The Field*
to whist correspondents, it really appears
as though some card-players never learn.
Week after week the same replies are giv-
en to the same questions asked, and many
of these questions are clearly and fully
dealt with in the laws, but do not seem to
be comprehended by the inquirers.

BETS

In the " Etiquette of Whist " it is stated :
" Until the players have made such bets as
they wish, bets should not be made with
outsiders."

In all the cases which follow the players
are referred to as A, B, Y, Z, as shown in
the following diagram.

```
        B
  ┌─────────────┐
  │             │
Y │             │ Z
  │             │
  │             │
  └─────────────┘
        A
```

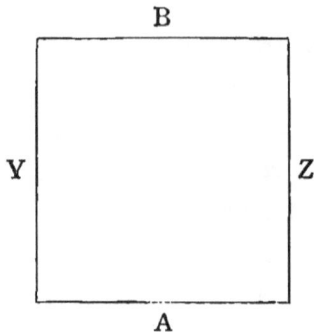

CASE 1.—A says while dealing, "I will bet ten shillings on the odd trick on this game." Y and Z make no remark. Before the turning up of the trump card, X, an outsider, says, "I will take your bet." Y says, "No, I claim the bet before a by-stander." X claims that neither Y nor Z accepted the bet, and so he is entitled to have it.

Decision.—As neither Y nor Z accepted the bet, it certainly seems that X's claim is just. It was only just previous to the turn-ing up of the trump card that X spoke; Y might have spoken some time previously, but did not do so. By the letter of the law Y may claim the bet, but it would certainly be bad form to do so.

CASE 2.—A bets on the odd trick when

he and his partner are at the score of two,
Y and Z being nothing. Y and Z win the
odd trick, but have revoked. A and B
add three to their score, and as the penalty
for the revoke takes the precedence of every
other score (Law 71, Section 5), A and B
win a treble. Y then claims to have won
the bet on the odd trick.

Decision.—This is a very interesting case.
As soon as A, B, add three to their score
the game is over, and it is a treble. If Y
and Z were allowed to score their trick
it might be claimed as only a double. Y
and Z no doubt won the trick, but by illegal
play, and they cannot score it. If sixpenny
points were being played, but a sovereign was
bet on the odd trick, Y, by revoking, might
win a sovereign, but there is no escape from
Law 80; A loses his bet on the odd trick.

CASE 3.—A with four cards in his hand
says, "I will bet a sovereign I win every
trick." He plays the twelfth trump (the
best). Z does does not follow suit, yet he
holds the thirteenth trump. A then plays
ace, king, queen of a plain suit; but Z trumps
one of these; so A does not win every trick,
and Z claims the bet.

Decision.—Z's play is dishonest, or, at least,

unfair (see " Etiquette of Whist "), and he not only deserves to lose the bet, but should not be permitted to play in future rubbers. Such proceedings, fortunately, are most uncommon.

CASE 4.—A bets with Y on the odd trick; Y and Z win two by cards, but revoke; A and B elect to take three tricks from Y and Z, and add these to their own tricks. Does A or Y win the bet on the odd trick?

Decision.—A wins; the score stands in accordance to the results after the penalty is enacted. (See Law 80; also Case 2. So, although Y Z won two by cards, yet when three tricks have been taken from them they lose two tricks.)

CASE 5.—A revokes; Y, at end of hand, says, " I will take three tricks from A's packet and add them to my own." " You can't do that," remarks A; "it is making a double penalty. I will bet five pounds you cannot." Y makes no remark, but leaves the room and brings in *Cavendish on Whist*, and shows A Law 72, by which Y's claim is correct. Y then says, " That is five pounds you owe me." " You never took the bet," remarks A. " You said nothing, and therefore it is no bet." Y claims it as a bet.

Decision.—Although the dispute is relative to a whist law, the question is one more nearly connected with the laws of betting. A offered a bet of five pounds, Y said nothing, neither did the other players, neither probably did a dozen bystanders. Each player and bystander might therefore claim five pounds. This is unfortunately a by no means uncommon proceeding with some persons; the bet is loosely made, and after the point is decided a claim is made or disputed. To have made this bet binding on A, Y before leaving the room should have said, "I feel certain I am right in my claim, and I accept your bet if you are equally certain;" an assent from A would then have made it a bet. To leave the room without speaking, and to look at the law in the book, gives a slight suspicion that it was a case of "If I'm right, I win five pounds; if wrong, it's no bet."

CARDS DETACHED (Law 60)

CASE 6.—-A took a card out of the rest of his hand, entirely separating it from his other cards; he then put it back, and prepared to play another card. Y said, "I call that card." "Name it," said A. "It is a court card in hearts," replied Y. "But you must name the card," said A. "I have named it," replied Y. Must A play the card?

Decision. — Certainly not. Y has not named the card.

CASE 7.—A took a card from his hand, then put it back. Y said, "I call that card." "Name it," said A. "The king of clubs," said Y. "I don't hold the king of clubs," said A. B won the trick, A won the next trick, Y won the third trick. "Now," said A to Y, "lead a heart." "You cannot call a lead from me now," said Y; "it is too late."

Decision.—Y's contention is childish; the law (60) says a suit can be called from Y or Z when he or his partner first have the lead.

CASE 8.—It is Y's lead, and he is obliged to lead a trump, as he holds only three cards, all trumps. Z turned up the king of trumps, which he still holds. A, fourth player, holds ace, queen, knave of trumps. A shows to Y the ace, then the queen, then the knave, and claims that all three tricks are his. Y claims these three cards as exposed, and in addition says, "You cannot win all three, if my partner plays a small trump and holds three trumps." How should this case be settled ?

Decision.—A, by detaching each card, rendered himself liable to have each card treated as an exposed card, and A's knave could be called on Z's king. When Y says, "If my partner play a small trump you cannot win the three tricks," he gives away his advantage, and commits a grave breach of etiquette, as he really tells his partner how to play. Under these conditions it seems only just that A's error should be condoned by Y's advice to his partner. It is very hard on Z, who, if he were really a whist player, would have divined the cards in A's hand, and would have known that A must win the trick, no matter what Z played. Z would therefore have played his smallest trump, and retained his king guarded to be led up to, as he no doubt would do. This anxiety to show winning cards is a common proceeding with some players, who really seem to imagine that holding high cards is a proof of great skill.

CARDS LIABLE TO BE CALLED
(Laws 56–66)

CASE 9.—A is third player; diamonds are led. When it is his turn to play, he plays the king and the eight of diamonds at the same time. Y, fourth player, calls the eight of diamonds, and wins with the ten; he then leads the ace, and calls the king. A says, "You cannot do that; it is enacting two penalties for one offence."

Decision.—It is curious how often this case is disputed or referred. By the American code, A might state he intended to play the king, and the eight remains an exposed card; but by the English code, if two cards are played at once, the adversaries have the right to call either to the current trick, and afterwards to call the other card (Law 56).

CASE 10.—A, in taking up his cards, drops one face upwards on the table; with great rapidity he places his hand over this card, and puts it among his other cards. Z says, "You must leave that card on the table" (see Law 56). A says, "I really don't know what the card was." Then says Z, "To the best of your belief you must place the card on the table." "I have no belief," says A;

" I don't even know the suit." What is the penalty ?

Decision.—On this case being referred to *The Field*, it was stated that A must, " to the best of his belief," place the card on the table. But A has no belief. A has really committed two offences : first, dropping a card face upwards on the table ; secondly, concealing the identity of the card by the rapid movement of his hand. Is he to escape from any penalty because he has no idea what the card is? If he did so, it would be a very dangerous precedent. If he were allowed to expose any card he chose, he might select the least damaging in his hand. If A were compelled to place his cards face downwards on the table, and one of the adversaries were to draw from his pack one card to be exposed, it would be the most simple solution of this difficulty.

CASE II. — The following is a frequent cause of disputes, and Cavendish, *On Whist*, has wisely dealt with it in Case V., from which the following is copied :

"Y throws down his cards, remarking, ' We have lost the game.' On this A and B (Y's adversaries) throw down their cards.

4

Z retains his hand. A and B plead that they were misled by Y, and that therefore they are not liable to Law 58." *

Decision.—A's, Y's, and B's hands are exposed, and must be left on the table to be called, each player's by the adversary. Z is not bound to abandon the game because his partner chooses to do so. Consequently Y's remark does not bind Z. A and B ought to keep up their cards until they have ascertained that both adversaries have abandoned the game.

CASE 12.—A takes up his cards, sorts them, and then places his cards in a packet face upwards on the table, only the top card is seen. What is the penalty?

Decision.—The conventional penalty for this offence is, that A's thirteen cards can be called. This penalty is, I think, very severe, and the only law that seems to warrant it is Law 56, Section 2, where a card dropped face upwards on the table is an exposed card.

As remarked by Cavendish, "Cases and Decisions:" "In a perfect whist code there

* The written law is sufficient to decide this case (*vide* Law 58); but inasmuch as the irregularity in question is a fertile source of disputes, the case has been deemed worthy of insertion.

should be a penalty for all errors or irregularities, by which the player committing them on his side *might* profit; and, on the other hand, there should be no penalty for errors by which he who commits them *cannot possibly* gain an advantage. Penalties should be proportioned as closely as possible to the gain which might ensue to the offender."

This being a principle of a perfect whist code, let us examine the offence in this case and the penalty. A places his cards face upwards on the table, but only the top card is exposed. The penalty is, that the whole of his thirteen cards can be called. Is this penalty proportioned as closely as possible to the gain which might ensue to the offender? What gain could possibly ensue to the offender by placing his cards face upwards on the table, when only one card out of the thirteen could be seen? What penalty could be more severe than that of calling the whole of his thirteen cards?

I anticipated that when the American whist code was made out this very severe penalty for so small an offence would have been corrected, but it has not been. Law 20, Section 1, "American Laws of Whist," states: "Every card faced upon the table otherwise than in the regular course of play, but not including a card led out of turn, is liable to be called." Hence, by this American law, the same penalty for exposing one card may be enacted, viz., the whole thirteen can be called. The penalty, therefore, of calling the whole thirteen cards, when only one can be seen, is in direct opposition to two fundamental principles of a perfect whist code, viz.:

I. A player *cannot possibly* gain an advantage by placing his cards face upwards on the table when only one of the thirteen can be seen.

II. The penalty, viz., calling the whole of the thirteen cards, is excessive, compared to the offence.

That the top card, which is seen, should be treated as an exposed card, is much more in accordance with justice. It is a pity that this penalty is still considered just in any whist code.

CARDS DROPPED

CASE 13.—A, in gathering his cards when dealt to him, drops one on the floor, but does not know he has done so. He plays the hand out to his last, viz., the twelfth card, and then says I have no card. What is the penalty.

Decision.—If A does not discover this deficiency until he has played to the first trick, he is answerable for any revoke he may have made (Law 46). If A discover he has only twelve cards before he plays to the first trick, he may refuse to play until he has thirteen cards, and search for the missing card must be made.

CASE 14.—Three hands have been played with a pack of cards, which is therefore proved to be perfect. After the fourth deal with this pack, A drops a card on the floor while sorting his hand. Without looking on the floor, A puts his hand on the floor and picks up a card, and places this among the others in his hand. Y and Z win three tricks; Y then lays down the four honors and claims game. A looks through his hand and says, "Oh no, you are not game. I have a blank card in my hand; it is an imperfect pack, and is a 'no deal.' I can't play with twelve cards and a blank bit of paper." How should this case be decided?

Decision. — Three hands having been played with the pack, previous to the deal in which this case occurred, the pack must have been perfect. A dropped one of his cards; he picked up what he supposed was the card he had dropped, but he picked up instead a blank card. If he had picked up a lucifer-match or an envelope instead of his dropped card, his condition would have been the same: he had only twelve cards in his hand, and a rectangular piece of blank pasteboard. Hence Law 46 seems to apply directly to this case.

One of the objects of whist laws is to prevent any player from obtaining an unfair advantage by carelessness.

A drops a card and picks up a blank card, which he may claim is the card he dropped, and which was dealt to him. As, however, the pack had been proved to be perfect by previous deals, and as this pack had not left the table, and no card had been dropped out of it previous to the fourth deal, it must be taken as perfect when the fourth deal was completed. A drops a card and picks up something else, and claims it is no deal, as he does not hold thirteen cards. How could the blank card possibly have found its way into a pack, and a card of that pack gone under the table. If the blank card had been in the pack when the deal occurred, then no doubt Law 37 would apply, as the pack was imperfect, and a new deal must be made. But as there is direct proof that the pack was perfect, while there is no proof that A picked up that which he had dropped, it seems opening the door to means of obtaining an unfair advantage through carelessness if there be no penalty except a new deal.

If a player, seeing he had no winning card in his hand, became quite indifferent, and dropped a card and picked up a dummy blank card, he would obtain a very unfair advantage if by doing so he could claim a fresh deal. The missing card from A's hand was found on the floor close to him when search was made; thus all the evidence seems to prove that A dropped that which he did not pick up. If A had not dropped a card, but immediately on taking up his hand had announced that he had twelve cards and a blank card, then the case would have been clear, and by Law 37 there must be a new deal. This incident shows how carefully and accurately all the facts of a case must be stated in order that a just decision should be given. Thus A might refer this case as follows :

I had twelve cards and a blank card, Y and Z hold four by honors and win the trick, and claim game. I show my blank card, and claim a new deal What is the law?

Decision.—There must be a new deal (Law 37).

CASE 15.—A, while sorting his hand, drops a card; this card falls face upwards on the edge of the table; but as the smaller portion of the card falls on the table, this card rebounds and falls under the table. " That's lucky," said A ; "as the card has fallen on the floor it cannot be called " (Law 56). Y and Z claim that the card fell face upwards on the table, and though it afterwards fell on the floor this does not release A from the penalty of having the card called.

Decision.—This case comes to a question of facts; the card did fall face upwards on the table, and if its face was sufficiently upwards to be seen by all the players, it must be considered as a card that fell face upwards on the table, the fact of its afterwards falling on the floor does not prevent it from having fallen face upwards on the table, and hence being an exposed card. The meaning of Law 56 evidently applies to cards dropped directly on the floor.

CASE 16.—A, in taking up his hand, drops a card, which fact nobody notices. After a few tricks have been won by Y and Z it is found that they hold no honors. The hands are however played out, and at the end it is found that Y is a card short. The missing card is one of the honors, and is found on the floor. Y and Z claim that there ought to be a fresh deal, and that A and B cannot score anything.

Decision.—If A in consequence of having dropped a card has revoked, he is liable for this, just as though the dropped card had been in his hand. If he has not revoked, any score A and B may have made holds good (Law 46).

CASE 17.—A is playing with a dummy against Y and Z ; a card from dummy's hand is dropped on the floor, its absence is not noticed till half the hand is played. What is the penalty?

Decision.—None. The card is restored to dummy's hand, and there is no penalty for any revoke which may have been made in consequence of the absence of this card.

CASE 18.—A playing with dummy drops the ace of clubs face upwards on the table, and is about to pick it up, when Z says,

" Leave that card on the table." A does so. When a club is led, Z calls on A to play the ace. A takes up the ace and plays the ten, which wins the trick. Z claims that this is not in accordance with whist law.

Decision.—It is not in accordance with whist law, but is in accordance with the laws of dummy. A cannot be called on to play the ace of clubs. A could not by any possibility gain an advantage by exposing his ace of clubs. Dummy being blind and deaf, A may expose all his cards.

It is curious how often I have known of such a penalty being claimed even by very old players.

CARDS EXPOSED

CASE 19.—A deals and turns up queen of spades, and allows this trump card to remain on the table after the second trick is turned and quitted. Y leads ace of spades at the third trick, and calls the queen of spades on the trick. A says, " Well, I will play it, but it's sharp practice," An opinion is requested.

Decision.—The whole question indicates the tyro, and shows that the disputants were very young. Rule 52 says that the trump card is liable to be called if left on the table after the *first* trick is turned and quitted. A left it till after the second trick was turned and quitted. Does A consider that if trumps had not been led he might have left his queen exposed till the eighth or ninth trick had been won? It is certainly not usual to call the trump card if left after the first trick is turned, but the rule positively states it may be called when so left. After the second trick it deserves to be called, even in order to cure A of such slack habits. Leaving the trump card exposed indicates negligence. The remark about sharp practice indicates a bad temper, and both are among the worst faults of a whist player.

By the American whist code a longer grace is given than by the English laws (Rule 18). The American code allows the trump card to remain on the table until the second trick has been played to ; if it remain on the table after the second trick has been turned and quitted, it is liable to be called. In England it has become a sort of conventional courtesy not to call the trump card, even if it remain on the table after the first trick is turned and quitted, yet it is liable to be called. Now comes a question which I have never seen occur or discussed; but as it may occur, it is worth considering.

The dealer leaves the trump card on the table until the first trick is turned and quitted. Law 52 states: "The dealer, when it is his turn to play to the first trick, should take the trump card into his hand; if left on the table after the first trick be turned and quitted, it is liable to be called; his partner may at any time remind him of his liability."

The wording of this law is certainly obscure. "All exposed cards are liable to be called" (Law 56). Then, if a card is liable to be called, is it not an exposed card?

If a partner may at any time remind the dealer of his liability to have the trump card called if he allow it to remain on the table, it would seem to indicate that by taking up the trump card his liability ceases, and this card cannot be treated as an exposed card. If Law 52 were as follows, there would be no obscurity:

The dealer, when it is his turn to play, should take the trump card into his hand. *As long as the trump card* remains on the table, after the first trick has been turned and quitted, it is liable to be called; his partner may at any time remind him of his liability.

CASE 20.—Y is a player who has the bad habit of picking up his cards as they are dealt to him one by one. A, who is dealing, in the hopes of breaking Y of this habit, deals a card to Y face upwards; the card thus exposed is a two. Y at once claims a new deal.

Decision.—Law 38 treats specially of such a case. Y, having touched his cards, cannot claim a new deal. The exposed card, however, cannot be called.

CASE 21.—A is dealing; Y during this deal reaches across the table to procure a match. One of the cards being dealt by A strikes Y's hand, and turns face upwards on the table. Can this be claimed as an exposed card, and can Y and Z claim a new deal?

Decision.—Y was in fault, and cannot claim a new deal. But as the card was actually exposed by Y, A may claim a new deal.

CARDS PLAYED IN ERROR

Numerous cases come under this head, and have been or will be dealt with in other portions of this work, but the following cases may help to impress the laws relative to this item on the memory of the whist-player:

CASE 22.—Towards the end of the hand Y leads the three of hearts, A (last player) at once plays the ace of hearts on the three before his partner, B, has played. Z says to B, "If you have no heart, trump that trick." Can Z compel B to trump?

Decision.—Rule 69 specially applies to this case. B must trump if he hold no heart, A, playing his ace before his partner has played, would indicate to B that he could win the trick; therefore if B were in doubt where the ace of hearts was, he might trump the heart, but when he sees his partner holds the ace, he would not do so unless compelled. If Z had played before B, then A might play his ace before his partner had played (Law 67).

CASE 23.—A is last player; B, his partner, plays a card higher than that led by Y, and which higher card cannot be topped by Z. A says, "Draw your cards," and, seeing the trick is his partner's, gathers up the three cards without playing a card to this trick. B leads, and A, third in hand, plays the ace of the suit led. Z says, " Well, I have a very bad hand, so I think I will have a new deal. Can Z claim a new deal ?

Decision.—Of course Z can. Rule 69 distinctly says so. If, however, Z and Y decided not to have a new deal, the extra card is considered to have been played to the imperfect pack, but does not constitute a revoke.

About this law there is a slight obscurity. Suppose A held ace, king, queen of trumps, and trumps were led. B plays ten, second hand, and Y cannot head the ten ; A gathers the three cards, and retains his ace, king, queen. B leads and A wins the trick, and then leads his ace, king, queen of trumps, which trumps we will suppose are spades. A then plays ace, king of another suit, which gives him the trick and two by honors. If A is at the score of two, the game would be won. On the hand being played out, A is found to have a card too many. Now Law 69 says, " If such error be not discovered until he has played to the next, the adversaries may claim a new deal." It would be more clear to state : If such error be not discovered until he has played to the next trick, the adversaries, *even at the end of the hand*, may claim a new deal. It too often happens that, when one side want only three to win the game, and have shown two by honors and win the trick, their adversaries throw down their cards. In such a case as the preceding, the fact of a player not having played to a trick might not be noticed. I cannot but think, however, that it is a great want of observation for any player to allow his partner to gather three cards, and not to play to this trick. But if this oversight be discovered *even at the end of the hand*, then the non-offending partners may apply Law 69. No doubt this is the meaning of Law 69; but I have seen many cases where a player having failed to play to a trick, and has then played again, has at once claimed that either a new deal must be claimed, or he must play a card from his hand to the imperfect trick. The offence is a serious one and might affect the game; hence the penalty ought to be serious. If the hand be played out, and the offending player score, say, three, he is severely punished by the adversaries demanding a new deal. If, however,

the non-offending players score three, they
may elect that the deal stand good. To
elect *at once*, when the default has been discovered, whether a new deal should be
made, does not seem to be giving a sufficient penalty for the offence.

There is another item connected with this
case which is worth considering. By Law
84, " Where a player and his partner have
an option of exacting from their adversaries
one of two penalties," they may not consult
as to which of these penalties is to be exacted,
except in the case of a revoke. In Law 69
it is stated, " should *they* decide that the deal
stand good." It is difficult to understand
how *they* could decide, unless they consulted.
It would certainly be just if in this case the
partners should be permitted to consult
whether a new deal should be claimed. But
no mention is made in the laws of the legal-
ity of this consultation ; in fact, by Law 84, if
a player say to his partner, " shall we have a
new deal," he loses all right to any penalty,
although Law 69 says, " should *they* decide."
I do not consider Law 69 quite as clear as
it might be. In Law 19 of the American
code this omission is made good. It is
there stated that the partners may con-

5

sult, and shall have the choice of a new deal or having the hand played out. Then, however, by the American code, comes that which seems to me a defect. Law 19 says, " If any player has a surplus card by reason of an omission to play to a trick, his adversaries can exercise the foregoing privilege only after he has played to the trick following the one in which such omission is made." If this law were as follows, I consider it would be more definite: " If any player has a surplus card by reason of an omission to play to a trick, his adversaries cannot exercise the above privilege until after he has played to the trick following the one in which such omission is made, but the adversaries may exercise this privilege, even when the hand has been played out." Thus, although the adversaries may discover the error immediately, the defaulter has played to the trick following that in which the omission is made. They may elect to play the hand out before they decide whether or not they demand a new deal. It may, however, be urged that this is a case in which there are not two penalties.

CASE 24.—A sorts his cards and finds he has thirteen ; but in playing fourth in hand to the first trick he plays two cards which stick together. After three or four other cards have been played, A finds he is a card short. He says, " Stop, I am a card short." He searches on the floor, but cannot find the missing card. He then counts the cards in the tricks he has won, taking four from the top packet, four from the next, and four from the third, he having only three tricks. His packets are very loosely put together, but it is then found that an extra card remains on the table. A says, by Rule 70 I can search this lower packet and restore the missing card to my hand. Y claims that there is no proof that the extra card was played to the first trick ; the tricks were so loosely packed that the extra card might belong to the second trick, and if it did, it would be difficult to decide which card should be restored to A's hand. What should be done ?

Decision.—This dispute shows the necessity of placing carefully each packet of four cards. The memory of the players ought to be able to decide how each trick was won, and hence what the extra card played by A must be. A is liable for any revoke (Rule 70) he may have made in consequence of playing this extra card. When it has been decided what the extra card is which A has played, he may take it into his hand, and it is not considered an exposed card. This law seems very liberal, because, unless A has revoked he escapes from any penalty, though he has really exposed a card.

CLAIMS FOR OFFENCES

CASE 25.—A being last player, plays a spade to a heart; he immediately says, "Oh, I have a heart." The trick is his partner's so far, and his partner's queen is the highest card on the table. A holds the knave, four, and a small heart. Y says, "You must win that trick." A replies, "I cannot." "Then play your highest," says Y. "You cannot now call my highest," says A.

Decision.—The difference between Law 76 and Law 86 is too often forgotten; for the above offence A could be called on to play his highest or lowest, not to win the trick; and it is now universally admitted that if an adversary claim a penalty to which he is not entitled, he loses his right to claim a penalty to which he was entitled; hence A can play his lowest heart, and his spade ceases to be an exposed card.

CASE 26.—A leads a heart, and each player follows suit, the trick being won by B. Before the cards are gathered, A plays another heart to the four already on the table, and proceeds to gather the five cards. B calls his partner's attention to this, and A states that he believed he had not played to this trick, and therefore played a heart. The adversaries claim that A has led out of turn.

Decision.—An exactly similar case is dealt with in Case 11, *Cavendish on Whist*, and is an undoubtedly sound decision, and is as follows : " A has not led out of turn ; he has merely exposed a card. The abstract principle pleaded by the adversaries is quite sound, but it does not apply to this case. A's word must be taken as correctly representing the fact that he played a second time to one trick."

CASE 27.—Z leads when it is B's turn to lead. He is stopped, and B leads ; Y wins the trick. A then says, " I will now call a suit." " Let me call the suit," says B. Y and Z claim that this is a consultation, and that A and B have thereby lost their right to exact any penalty.

Decision.—This is not a consultation dealt with under Law 84. Partners may not by that law consult as to which of two penalties shall be exacted. They ought to agree which of the two shall exact the penalty. As, however, A said without consulting his partner, " I will now call a suit," the adversaries may insist on A calling a suit, and can object to B calling it.

CASE 28.—A, on looking over his hand, says, " I don't think it's any use your playing, as I have game in my hand." Z claims that A must place his cards face upwards on the table to be called.

Decision.—There is no penalty for saying, " I have game in my hand," by the English code ; it is merely a silly and impatient remark, which rarely saves time, and not unfrequently causes a revoke. If A has game in his hand, he can very soon prove the fact by playing his cards in the usual way. By the American code (Law 37) such a remark would entitle the adversaries to demand that the partner's hand be laid on the table and each card called.

CASE 29.—A and B are at the score of nothing, Y and Z are two, and hold two by honors. A and B win three by cards, but A has revoked. "Now, partner," says Y, "we will take two of A's tricks, and we will add one to our score; then we count our honors, and that makes us a double, as A and B will be only the trick." Z agrees to this. A and B claim that by Law 72, Section 4, this penalty is illegal, as the penalty for the revoke cannot be divided; hence, as Y and Z attempted to claim an illegal penalty, they have forfeited their claim to *any* penalty.

Decision.—By an unwritten but well-established custom players who, for an offence, claim a penalty to which they are not entitled, lose their right to claim the penalty to which they were entitled. Hence Y and Z cannot claim for the revoke. This case shows the absolute necessity of thoroughly understanding the written laws of whist.

CASE 30.—A is fourth player; hearts having been led, A plays a spade to the heart, but immediately says, "Stop, I have a heart." He waits a short time to see if the adversaries make any remark, and then wins the trick with the best heart. Z then says, "Now lead your spade." A claims that, as the spade is merely an exposed card, he cannot be called on to lead it, and that Z's claim is illegal in calling a lead.

Decision.—Z's claim is correct. It is surprising how often such an unsound objection as the above is urged against calling an exposed card when this constitutes leading the card. The exposed card can be called at any time, and calling this card is a very different thing from calling a lead. When a lead is called the offending player may be required to play *any* suit; but when the exposed card is called, though it happens to be the offending player's turn to lead, it is merely calling the exposed card.

CUTTING

CASE 31.—It is Y's deal; the cards with which Y is to deal are between Y and A. A cuts the cards for Y to deal, but Y does not touch the pack. A then says, " It's unlucky you did not claim my partner's revoke." Y and Z then remember that B revoked. Y says, " We can claim the revoke now." "No," says A, " not after the cards are cut for the next deal " (Law 78). " But," says Y, "you cut the cards before I presented them to you to be cut; it is therefore an illegal cut, which does not bar the claim for the revoke."

Decision.—Y's claim is sound; the pack ought to be presented by Y to be cut by A. The fact of A cutting them before Y had presented them renders the cut illegal. If Y had accepted the cut, and had reunited the two portions of the pack, and had commenced to deal, then it would have been too late to claim the revoke. If Y or Z had revoked, the fact of A cutting would have prevented this revoke from being claimed.

CASE 32.—Y shuffles the pack, and, it being his deal, places the pack for A to cut. A cuts the pack; Y reunites the two portions of the pack, and holds these in his hand while he discusses with his partner the play of the former hand. He then shuffles the pack, and again presents it to A to cut. A refuses to cut again, and claims that Y has lost his deal. Y says, " I merely forgot you had cut ; it is no matter, cut again." A refuses.

Decision.—Y shows ignorance of the laws. By Law 36 he loses his deal.

CASE 33.—A cuts the cards for Y to deal ; the packet he cut off he lifts very high, and in putting it on the table he drops and exposes the bottom card, which is an ace. He immediately claims there must be a fresh cut. Y claims that the option of a fresh cut belongs to him or his partner, and that he will accept the cut.

Decision.—Law 34 states: " If in cutting a card be exposed, there must be a fresh cut." Thus by this law A's contention seems to be justified ; but as it was the bottom or future turn-up card which was exposed, and by A's careless act, it seems unjust that Y should lose the benefit of having an ace cut in consequence of A's proceeding. Law 34 evidently refers to a card in the pack being exposed, and though the bottom card that was dropped may, by the letter of the law, be claimed as in the pack, yet this would be to inflict on Y an injury. A cut the pack, and cut his adversaries an ace ; then by a clumsy proceeding of his own he exposes this ace, and claims to deprive his adversaries of the benefit of holding it on account of his own default. As remarked by Cavendish : " The point kept in view throughout being that no player shall be allowed to profit by his own wrongdoing." If A were allowed to cut again, the chances would be twelve to one against his cutting an ace ; therefore he would be allowed to profit by his own wrong-doing. If, then, this case be decided by the letter of the law, then by Law 34 there must be a fresh cut. If it be decided by the general spirit of the law, then Y ought to have the option of the cut holding good. I believe that with players who adopt the principle of justice more than that of a cast-iron rule, it would be admitted that Y had the option of accepting the cut.

CASE 34.—A, B, C, D, Y, Z enter a card-room together. The cards are spread out, and are drawn as follows: A a three, B a four, C a king, D a ten, Y an ace, Z a six. A says, " C and D are out, and I and Y are partners." " No," says B, " we must cut again to decide who are partners ; we were merely cutting to decide who played the first rubber." A disputes this.

Decision.—This dispute, which has several times occurred in my own experience, is due solely to ignorance of the written laws. Law 16 states clearly : " The four who cut the lowest cards play first, and again cut to decide on partners."

CASE 35.—In cutting for partners, A cuts a ten, B, Y, and Z each cut a king. B, Y, Z cut again ; B cuts an ace, Y a two, and Z a nine. B claims that he and Y are partners, and have the choice of cards and seats.

Decision.—B is in error. Law 19 fully meets the case. A is the original lowest, and his partner is B. A has choice of cards and seats, and he deals.

CASE 36.—A, B, Y, Z enter a club card-room and cut for partners. A deals, and during the deal C enters the room and says, "I thought I should have been in time to cut." C then walks out of the room. In two hands A and B win a bumper. C is not in the room, so A says, "What are we to do?" "Cut again for partners, I suppose," said Y. They cut, and A and Y are now partners. They take their seats and A commences dealing, when C again enters the room, and remarks that he has been cut out of the rubber, and that it was a hard case. An opinion is requested.

Decision.—A, B, Z, Y were not bound to go in search of C. He left the room without any directions to the players. If he ran the risk of staying away long enough for the rubber to be won, he ought to have asked one of the players to draw a card for him for the next rubber, and also asked that he might be sent for. The whole dispute is due to C's negligence, and the four players cannot be accused of making a hard case for him, as he never even intimated that he would play in the next rubber.

CASES RELATIVE TO THE DEAL OR MISDEAL

CASE 37.—A in dealing turns up a card face upwards; he turns it face dowwards so quickly that neither Z nor Y knows what the card was. They ask A what the card was which was exposed, and in his partner's pack. A asserts he is not compelled to name it.

Decision.—A's proceeding is an attempt at unfairness. He must have seen the card, and thus knows one card in his partner's hand, and yet he refuses to give the information obtained by his own clumsy dealing to his adversaries. A is not warranted in concealing from the adversaries the value of the exposed card, and thus not giving the adversaries the option of a fresh deal.

CASE 38.—A in dealing turns up a card face upwards, but turns it face downwards so quickly that neither Y nor Z could name the card. Y claims that A must state what the card was, so that he may elect whether he have a new deal. A states he has not any knowledge of what the card was. B also states he did not see the card, and has no idea what it was. What is to be done?

Decision.—This case is similar in some respects to Case 10. A's statement that he has no knowledge of what the card is must be taken with *bona-fides*. None of the players saw the card, and though A undoubtedly committed an offence, it was one that under the conditions of no one seeing the card could not possibly give him an advantage. Yet by Law 56, Section 2, the card was an exposed card, though no one can name it. Then by Law 38, Y and Z can claim a new deal. Whether or not they would gain any advantage by doing so is doubtful; but to compel A to deal again might make him more cautious. At the same time it might be pointed out to A that snatching and turning over, face downwards, a card that he has exposed, is not a correct proceeding.

CASE 39.—A commences his deal by dealing two cards to Y and one to B. He takes the lower of the two cards that he has dealt to Y, and places this midway between the

other two cards, and says : " I am not bound
to deal each packet exactly in front of each
player ; the card on my left belongs to Y,
the centre card to B, and the other card to
Z, and I have altered the position of one
card only ; so it is not a misdeal, and I now
deal a card to myself. If I had made this
mistake after dealing one round, of course
I should have had to alter the position of
two cards, and it would have been a misdeal." Y claims that it is a misdeal.

Decision.— A's is an ingenious quibble ;
his argument that because he has altered
the position of only one card it is not a
misdeal is overruled by Law 44, Section 6,
viz.: "Should the dealer deal two cards at
once, or two cards to the same hand, and
then deal a third," it is a misdeal.

CASE 40.—A deals, but the trump card
comes to the hand on the left of the dealer.
The dealer claims this hand as his own, and
asks each of the players to count the packet
nearest to him. Each player does so, and
finds thirteen cards in each packet. A
claims that the deal holds good.

Decision.—It is a misdeal (see also Case
4, Cavendish.)

CASE 41.—A deals, and has just turned

up the trump card, but has not quitted it, when Z says, " Stop, it is my deal." "Too late," says A ; " I have turned the trump card." " But I stopped you before you quitted it," says Z ; "therefore I am in time."

Decision.—This case is somewhat similar to a claim for honors, made after the trump card of the following deal has been turned face upwards, but is not quitted. The exact angle at which a card is sufficiently turned to be called a turned-up card may be a frequent cause of dispute ; but there can be no dispute about a card being turned and *quitted.* Hence it is now universally admitted that the trump card must be turned and quitted to deprive the claimants of their right to score honors. The same arguments seem to apply to the claim for an erroneous deal. A not having turned and *quitted* the trump card, Z is in time to claim his deal.

CASE 42.—A while dealing deals a card to Z with such force that this card would have gone off the table had not Z stopped the card with his hand, and pushed it among his other cards. During the same deal A exposes an ace in his partner's pack. " A new deal," claims Z. "You can't claim a new deal," says A, "as you touched one of your cards."

Decision.—By the letter of the Law 38 A is correct, but under the circumstances A's claiming that Z touched his cards when he merely prevented one from falling on the floor is a proceeding not likely to produce any wish on the part of the other players to again join a rubber in which A is one of the players.

CASE 43.—A deals, but the trump card comes to his right adversary. A misdeal is claimed, and Y commences to deal. When Y has dealt fourteen cards, A says, " Stop, I am almost certain I did not misdeal ; I must count the pack." Y waits, and A counts fifty-two cards in the pack in which he had misdealt. "It's all right," said A; "I did misdeal." Y continues his deal, but deals the next card to his left adversary, and consequently misdeals. A claims this as a misdeal ; but Y claims he must deal again as he was interrupted.

Decision.—Law 50 applies specially to this case ; Y may deal again. If A had established his claim it would have been different.

CASE 44.—A deals and has dealt fifteen
6

cards, when he has a fit of sneezing ; he stops dealing till he has recovered. When he is about to continue his deal, B, his partner, says, " Deal the next card to yourself." Z claims that B has no right to tell his partner where he should place the next card.

Decision.—B may inform his partner. A player has as much right to prevent his partner from making a misdeal as he has to prevent him from revoking or leading out of turn.

CASE 45.—A cuts the cards for Y to deal. Y picks up the two portions of the pack sideways, and A sees the king of clubs at the bottom, which would become the trump card. A says, " I must cut again, as you have exposed the king of clubs at the bottom of the pack." Y claims that this is not an exposed card, as no one but A could have seen it.

Decision.—The king of clubs, having been seen and named by A, is an exposed card, and by Rule 34 A is entitled to cut again. If the pack when cut be united with one hand only, and the pack be lifted horizontally, the bottom card cannot well be exposed (see note on the "Deal," *Art of Practical Whist*).

CASE 46.—B, by consent of the adversaries, deals for A. He commences by dealing a card to Z, then to A, then to Y. Z and Y claim a misdeal, as B, dealing for A, ought to have dealt the first card to Y. B says, "It is no matter; I will shift each packet over to the other side." Z and Y still claim a misdeal.

Decision.—By Law 44, Section 1, it is a misdeal. B, although practically dealing, is really acting for A; to deal, therefore, the first card to Z is the same thing as though A did so. This penalty, however, is rarely claimed.

CASE 47.—A deals, but instead of turning up and quitting the trump card he places it on the table by itself face downward, quits it, and says, "Would any one like a bet on this rubber?" Y claims that the trump card being placed face downward on the table is an act which constitutes a misdeal.

Decision.—It is not a misdeal if the trump card did not touch any of the other cards that had been dealt.

CASE 48.—A and B were partners. A dealt, and his deal was so slovenly that he took up one of his partner's cards with his own; he thus held fourteen cards, his part-

ner twelve. The adversaries having each
thirteen, had no means of knowing the state
of their adversaries' hands. A won the first
trick; he then played ace, king, of a plain
suit, and laid down the four honors in
trumps and claimed game. He and his
partner, as well as their adversaries, threw
their cards on the table, when they were all
mixed, and their adversaries never had a
chance of discovering the defects in A and
B's hands. On the second occasion four
other players were playing, when a similar
occurrence took place, with the exception
that A and B (A being the dealer who took
up one of his partner's cards) held no winning cards, while Z and Y held two by honors, and won three by cards. But towards the
end of the hand A announced that he had
four cards in his hand, and his partner only
two, so, by Rule 44, it was a misdeal, and Z
and Y can score nothing. So that A's carelessness prevented Z and Y scoring game.
Is there no penalty for such an offence?

Decision.—As the laws at present stand,
Z and Y in the first case might have requested A and B to lay their remaining
cards on the table, when, by counting, they
would have discovered that one must have

held fourteen, the other only twelve cards;
consequently, A and B were not entitled to
score anything. In the second case there
was no remedy. It was a hard case that Z
and Y, by a fault of A, should not be allowed
to score their game. Still, such is the law
at present. I cannot but think that additional legislation on this point might be
made, and probably in the following manner: The dealer is responsible that he deals
thirteen cards to each player. Each player
must be responsible that he hold no more
and no less than thirteen. If two partners
hold twenty - six cards between them, one
holding more, the other less than thirteen,
while the adversaries hold thirteen each, no
score made by the partners holding the un-
equal number of cards can be counted in
that hand; whereas any score made by the
partners holding thirteen each can be counted. Such a law would at once meet the
case, the three cards in the last part of the
hand—viz., three in, say, A's hand—being
played so that one of these is allotted to B.
Hence, there would result a heavy penalty
for playing with fourteen cards in one hand
and twelve in the partner's. By the American code, Law 19, this injustice seems to be

remedied under the heading, " Irregularities in the hands."   The American Law 19 is as follows :

" If at any time after all have played to the first trick, the pack being perfect, a player is found to have either more or less than his correct number of cards and his adversaries have their right number, the latter, upon the discovery of such surplus or deficiency, may consult, and shall have the choice—

" I. To have a new deal.
" II. To have the hand played out, in which case the surplus, or missing card or cards, are not taken into account."

In the first edition of *The Art of Practical Whist*, published seventeen years ago, I put forward the suggestion (Case 19) given in the last " Decision " (Case 48).   This the Americans have adopted.   Hence, in such a case as that given in 48, where Z and Y, holding two by honors and winning three by cards, can score nothing, because B took up one of his partner's cards, by the American code Z and Y, who have committed no fault, could score game.   The American code is just ; the English code is unjust.   .

Then, again, by the American code, " If either of the adversaries also has more or less than his correct number, there must be a new deal." Both sides being in fault, this appears the only solution of the difficulty.

CASE 49.—A commences to deal, but misdeals. Does this misdeal count as a deal, as regards barring a claim for honors ? .

Decision.—This case occurred at the club at Simla in 1877. As an outsider the case was referred to me. I gave it as my opinion that a misdeal was no deal, and did not invalidate the scoring of honors. The case was much discussed, and was referred home. The decision, however, of the home authorities was not as decisive as it should or might have been. The reason why a misdeal should not be considered as a deal, when honors are to be counted, is the rapidity with which a misdeal may be made. Suppose A and B held honors, but have not named them when the cards are cut for the next deal. They see there is plenty of time to call and score them before the trump card is turned and quitted ; but Y, the dealer, deals the first two cards to his left adversary and the third card to his partner, and thus completes a misdeal with the first three cards, and if a misdeal were to count as a deal, then A and B would, in consequence of Y's fault and act, be deprived of their right to score honors—a result which cannot be just, and cannot therefore be law. Hence, I think it always ought to be decided that a misdeal does not prevent honors from being claimed. It is now universally admitted that a misdeal is not a bar to claiming honors. If it were, it might be rewarding an adversary for a blunder.

CASE 50.—The cards are cut for A to deal. A unites the two packets, and looks at the bottom or trump card. Y claims that this constitutes a misdeal.

Decision.—It does not. By Law 41 the adversaries may see the bottom card and may claim a new cut or deal. By the American code, Law 17, Section 5, it is a misdeal if the dealer look at the trump card before he has completed his deal.

CASE 51.—A deals. At the completion of the deal one card is midway between Y's and B's packet of cards. Y says to A, "Is that card mine or your partner's?" B says he is uncertain. "Then," says Y, "you must allot it either to me or your partner, or else I claim a misdeal."

Decision.—This is one of the cases where A can gain no possible advantage by dealing a card midway between the pack of an adversary and of his partner; and though the dealer is bound to deal thirteen cards to each player, the act of dealing a card in the manner stated above is usually treated liberally, and in the following manner: Y and B count their cards; the doubtful card is then taken up by the player who holds twelve cards only.

CASE 52.—The first hand dealt with a new pack of cards reveals the fact that there are fifty-three cards in the pack. The backs of the cards are alike, and no dummy card is found in the pack. To lay out the pack in suits takes a long time, and requires much shuffling to readjust the pack. Is there any more rapid manner of finding what is the surplus card?

Answer.—Yes. Turn the pack face upwards and count the pips on the top card. Suppose this card is an 8; place this card on the table and count the pips on the next card and add these pips to 8; suppose the second card is a 7, then 8 and 7 make 15; subtract 10, and there remains 5; add the pips on the next card to 5; say the next card is a 4, then

5 and 4 make 9; add the pips on a third card to 9; say the next card is a 3, then 9 and 3 make 12; subtract 10, and 2 remains; and so proceed throughout the pack. Whenever a 10 or a court card comes, place this on the table without counting it. Having arrived at the end of the pack, the number over, say 4, shows that the extra card is a 4; if the number over be 8, the extra card is an 8; and by running through the pack it can easily be seen in which suit there are two 4's or two 8's. If nothing be over, the extra card will be a 10 or a court card, which can easily be detected. If a card be missing from a pack, adopt the same method of counting, but at the end subtract the number over from 10, and the remainder will indicate the pips on the missing card. Any person fairly quick in adding will accomplish this performance in less than two minutes; whereas, to arrange the cards in suits will occupy at least five or six minutes, and will, unless shuffled thoroughly, cause the cards to lump in suits in the next deal.

CASE 53.—A, during his deal, finds the ace of spades faced in the pack. This ace is dealt to Y. " I will accept the ace," says Y;

" we won't have a fresh deal." " We must,"
says A.

Decision.—During a long whist experience I have several scores of times found
Y's contention urged. Law 37, Section 2,
states, "There must be a new deal." That
which was probably passing through the
mind of Y was that when a dealer turns up
a card and exposes it the adversaries may, if
they chose, claim a new deal (Law 38).

CASE 54.—During the deal A deals two
cards to Y. He takes the top card of the
two and gives this to B. Y claims this as a
misdeal, as A took the wrong card and gave
this to B.

Decision.—It is a misdeal.

CASES RELATIVE TO EXPOSED CARDS

CASE 55.—A plays two cards, a small
heart and a small spade, to a heart led. B
wins this trick, and leads the king of spades.
A's small spade is of course an exposed card,
and he plays this to his partner's king. Y
objects, and says, " We won't have that
card now; you must play another spade.
We intend to call that exposed card pres-
ently." A claims that his adversaries can-

not prevent him from playing his exposed card.

Decision.—It is surprising how often this erroneous claim is made. A can of course play his exposed card to his partner's king. The adversaries cannot prevent him from getting rid of his exposed card.

CASE 56.—A leads a small diamond when it is Y's lead. He is going to take up this diamond when Z says, " Leave that down ; it is an exposed card." Y leads a heart, which A wins. " Now," says Z, " lead a club." " You cannot call a lead from me now," says A, " because you claimed my diamond as an exposed card ; you can only call my diamond."

Decision.—This error of A's is very common. He is correctly told that his diamond is an exposed card, and must be left on the table ; but this fact does not prevent Z from calling a lead from A or B when it is next the turn of either to lead. A's offence was not exposing a card, but leading out of turn. Y and Z have the option of calling the exposed card, or calling a lead (Law 62). A, being told that his small diamond was an exposed card, is merely telling him a fact, but does not prevent Y or Z from calling a lead.

CASE 57.—A leads a diamond when it is Y's lead. Y leads a club, and Z says, "If you have no club play that diamond." A wins the trick with the best club. Z then says, "Now lead a heart." "You cannot call a lead now," says A, "as you have elected to call my diamond as an exposed card."

Decision.—By Law 84 A is correct; and by the established but unwritten law Z, having attempted to claim a penalty to which he was not entitled, loses his claim to any penalty; he cannot therefore call A's diamond as an exposed card.

CASE 58.—A heart is led by Y. B plays a small heart, Z plays the queen, A plays the two. A then says, "Stop; I intended to play my king." Y claims the king of hearts as an exposed card.

Decision.—The king of hearts having been named by A is as much an exposed card as though it had been placed face upward on the table.

CASE 59.—A exposes the three of spades; Y, whose lead it is, plays a small heart; B plays a small heart; Z heads the trick with the ten, and calls the three of spades. A then takes the three of spades and places it in his hand. Z says, "Leave that card on the table; it is an exposed card." A says, "You have called it once; you cannot call it again, and I have a heart."

Decision.—This error of A's is very common. Law 65 says: "The call of a card can be repeated (at every trick) until such card has been played."

CASE 60.—B sorts his cards, and then places the pack face upward on the table. Can all his thirteen cards be called?

Decision.—Yes. See also Case 12.

CASE 61.—B deals, and leaves the trump card on the table till after the first trick is turned and quitted. Z wins the first trick and leads a trump, and when B attempts to take up the trump card Z objects, and claims that it is an exposed card, and that his sole object in leading a trump was to call B's trump card.

Decision.—By Law 52 Z can call the trump card, but it is not usual to do so. Hence, this law should not be rigidly enforced.

CASE 62.—B deals, and turns up the king of diamonds. After three tricks have been won A says, "What are trumps?" B replies, "You ought to remember; I turned up the king of diamonds." Y and Z claim that the king of diamonds having been named is an exposed card and must be laid on the table. B claims that now Y and Z have lost their right to claim any penalty, as they have attempted to claim a wrong one.

Decision.—By Law 53, B, having named the trump card, is liable to have his highest or lowest trump called. He cannot be made to place this card on the table as an exposed card. Hence, Y and Z attempted to enforce an illegal penalty, and consequently cannot afterwards claim any penalty.

CASE 63.—B deals, and immediately Z leads B takes the trump card in his hand. Before Y plays he says, "I want to see the trump card." "I forget what it is," says B. Y wins the first trick, a spade; leads a second spade, which Z wins. Z leads a third spade, on which A plays a winning spade. "Now," said Z, "if you have no spade, trump that with your best trump." B declares that he cannot be compelled to trump as desired.

Decision.—B, by Rule 55, must trump with his best trump if he hold no spade. Though the written law (55) is clear on this case, I have known scores of such cases, even with players who have played whist during upward of thirty years, who, like B, have asserted that they could not be compelled to play their best trump.

CASE 64.—Y deals, and turns up the three of diamonds. B leads a spade. Just as Z is playing Y takes up the trump card. Before A plays, B says, "I want to see the trump card." Y says, "I forget it." B wins the first trick, and leads the two of diamonds (trumps), Z plays the four, A plays the five, and, remembering that the three was turned, calls on Y to play his lowest trump. Y disputes.

Decision.—By Law 55 Y can be called on to play his highest or lowest trump, and A's is a legal claim.

CASE 65.—Y takes the trump card into his hand before he is legally entitled to do so, and states that he forgets what it is. He wins the first trick. A then says, "Lead your best trump." Y claims that this is an illegal claim, as a lead cannot be called.

Decision.—This is the oft-repeated dispute about calling an exposed card when it constitutes a lead. Y's highest or lowest trump can be called at any time during the hand, even though it is Y's lead. Many players fail to perceive the absurdity of their objection to a card being called when it constitutes a lead. In some cases the offending player might escape from any penalty. Thus, suppose Y held ace, king, queen, and a two of trumps, and exposed the two, and it was Y's lead. If the two could not be called because it was Y's lead, he might lead his ace, king, queen, and probably draw all the trumps except his own two; whereas, if he played the two as a lead, A might win the trick. Y, failing to remember the trump card, causes his highest or lowest trump (according as the adversaries elect) to occupy the position of an exposed card, which can be called at any time, as long as playing it does not constitute a revoke.

FORMATION OF TABLE

CASE 66.—A, B, C are in the card-room waiting for a rubber. D enters the room and is asked by A if he will make up a rubber. D replies, "No, thank you." E then enters the room and accepts the invitation to make up the rubber; but D then says, "I claim to play in this rubber, as I was in the room before E." A, B, C will not admit D's right to play in the first rubber, as he

7

declined to do so when asked. D says his reason for declining was because he objected to play in a set rubber of only four players, but now that there are five he will play.

Decision.—It is difficult to legislate for the proceedings of cranks; but in this case D, having once refused to make up the rubber, leaves the fourth place vacant, and E ought certainly to be the fourth player in the first rubber.

CASE 67.—A, B, C enter the card-room somewhat early in the afternoon. As there is no fourth to make a rubber, they agree to play with a dummy until a fourth player arrives, and to stop immediately a rubber can be made up. After about half an hour four players, D, E, F, G, enter the card-room, and, seeing that A, B, C are playing, D says, " We four can now cut for partners for our rubber." B objects, and claims that A, B, C being first in the room, and having waited half an hour for a rubber, have a right to play in the first rubber, and that D, E, F, G must cut to see who is to make the fourth player. D claims that by Law 22 D, E, F, G have a right to play the first rubber, and that A, B, C must cut in order to decide which of the two complete the table.

Decision.—Dummy is not considered the same thing as whist. If A, B, C had amused themselves by playing "beggar my neighbor," or any other game, even dummy, this playing does not bar their claim to play in the first rubber. D, E, F, G each cut a card; the highest, say D, is out of the first table. E, F, G then cut, and whoever cuts the lowest card joins A, B, C for the first rubber. Suppose E to have cut the lowest card, then A, B, C, E cut for partners and play the first rubber.

CASE 68.—Referring to the last case, D, F, and G are not playing in the first rubber when H and J enter the room, and propose that the five players cut to form a second table.

Decision.—D, F, G being first in the room are entitled to be in the second table; having also cut for the first table, they have an additional right. H and J must cut, and the cutter of the lower card plays with D, F, G the first rubber in the second table.

CASE 69. — A, an old gentleman, enters the club door, and ascends slowly the stairs leading to the whist-room. B, a young man, enters the club door after A, and runs up the stairs two steps at a time past A, and enters the card-room before A, and announces his intention of joining a rubber, which, before his arrival, had five players belonging to the table. On A entering the card-room he finds the table complete with six players, and he is deprived of playing a rubber during the whole afternoon.

Decision.—This is not a solitary case of the bad manners sometimes shown by the rising generation. A should state what occurred to the other players. Perhaps in future it might be wise for A to provide himself with a heavy stick the breadth of the stairs, and while ascending these to hold the stick horizontal so as to prevent any one passing him.

HIGHEST OR LOWEST CARD; WHEN IT CAN BE CALLED

Many mistakes from want of a knowledge of the laws are made as regards this penalty.

CASE 70.—Y leads a small spade; A at once plays king of spades; before B or Z have played, Z says to B, "Play your highest spade." "You need not do so," says A.

Decision.—Z's claim is illegal. B can be called on to win or not to win the trick (see Law 68), but he cannot be called on to play his highest or lowest.

CASE 71.—Y leads four of spades, B plays ten of spades, Z plays three of spades; A hesitates before playing, and B says, "It's mine, partner." Z says to A, "Play your highest spade." B objects, and says, "A can be called on to win or not to win the trick, but cannot be made to play his highest."

Decision.—Z's claim is correct (Law 86).

CASE 72.—Y leads three of diamonds, B plays knave of diamonds, Z plays six of diamonds. Before A has played B draws his knave of diamonds towards him to show this card is his. Z requests A to play his highest diamond. Can A be compelled to do so?

Decision.—Certainly (see Law 86).

CASE 73.—Y leads two of hearts, B plays six of hearts, Z plays eight of hearts; before A plays B says, "It's against you, partner." Z calls on A to play his lowest heart. B objects, and says he "neither named his card, said it was his, nor drew his card towards him."

Decision. — B's remark is equivalent to drawing his card, and Law 86 applies.

HONORS SCORING

CASE 74.—The following is Case 2 in Cavendish, and is, as he remarks, "a good instance of interpretation in accordance with the spirit of the law :" A and B claim "the game" and score it. After the trump card of the following deal is turned up, Y and Z object that A and B have not claimed honors (*vide* Laws 6 and 7).

Decision.—The honors were claimed within the meaning of the law. The objection to the score, if made really in ignorance of how it accrued, should have been taken at once. Y and Z should not wait the completion of the deal, so as to entrap A and B on a mere technicality.*

CASE 75.—A and B win two by cards and hold two by honors. During the next deal they discuss the play of the hand, and before the trump card is turned A says to B,

---

* This is a good instance of interpretation in accordance with the spirit of the law. Laws should never be so construed as to inflict a wholly unnecessary wrong, as would happen in this case were the law insisted on literally. The intention of Law 7 is to require A and B to draw attention to the claim, and this is sufficiently done by the claim of "the game."

"Score four." Y turns up the trump card, and then says, "What are you scoring?" "Two by cards and two by honors," replies A. "You never called your honors," remarks Y, "and scoring them is not sufficient."

Decision.—Case 2 in Cavendish applies to this case. How could A and B be four unless they intimated that the extra two above their tricks were honors. Y should have questioned the score before he turned the trump card if he were really in doubt as to how the score was made up. To wait until he has turned up the trump card indicates a desire to entrap the adversaries on a mere technicality.

CASE 76.—A and B hold two by honors; they do not name or score them until after the cards have been cut for Y to deal, and Y misdeals. "Why did you not count your honors?" asks Z. "We will count them now," replies A. "Too late; my partner has dealt," says Z. "No," says A; "he misdealt."

Decision.—A misdeal is not a deal, and does not bar the claim for honors (see Case 49).

CASE 77.—A and B, at the commence-

ment of a deal, are at the score of four; Y
and Z are nothing. Y and Z win the trick.
A and B hold two by honors, but A has revoked. Y and Z elect to deduct three
from A and B's score, and make the game
one all. A then claims he can score his
two by honors, as he is at the score of one.

Decision.—A cannot score his honors (see
Law 4): "Those players who, at the commencement of a deal, are at the score of
four, cannot score honors."

CASE 78.—A and B are at the score of
three. They win the trick and hold two
by honors, but they have revoked. Y and
Z are nothing. After a long consultation Y
and Z elect to take three tricks from A and
B, and claim that this will make the game
stand three all. A says, "We can count our
honors now, though we cannot score game;
we can score as far as four. So the game
stands four to your three." Z says, "You
cannot count one by honors; there is no
such thing."

Decision.—A and B count two by honors,
but can only score as far as four.

CASE 79.—A and B hold four by honors,
lose the trick, and revoke. Can Y and Z
exact any penalty by which A and B can be

prevented from scoring as far as four. The game is love all.

Decision.—No. In whatever way the penalty is exacted the game will stand four all.

CASE 80.—A and B win the trick and hold two by honors; they score the trick, and Y goes on with the deal. Just as Y is about to turn up the trump card, A says, " Stop ; are we not two by honors?" Before it is agreed that A and B were two by honors Y turns up and quits the trump card, and claims that it is too late to score honors.

Decision.—Immediately a question as to A and B holding honors was raised, Y should have waited before turning up the trump card till the question was settled. A requested Y to stop, but Y did not comply with this request. The fact of Y hurrying on with the deal during the discussion about honors does not prevent honors from being counted.

CASE 81.—A deals and turns the trump card face upward, but retains it in his hand, and says, "We are two by honors, partner; you had better score them." " Too late," says Z ; "the trump card is turned up " (see Law 6).

Decision.—See Case 41. It is not too late.

CASE 82.—The following is Case 1 in Cavendish: The play of the hand shows that A and B (partners) hold no honor. The hand is therefore abandoned, and the adversaries (Y and Z) score the game. It is then discovered that Y has only twelve cards, and one of the honors is found on the floor. A and B then object to the score on the ground that Y and Z only "held" three honors (*vide* Law 3).

Decision.—Y and Z are entitled to score four by honors. Y is not obliged to play with his cards in his hand. Besides, the game having been abandoned, Law 59 comes into operation. The penalty for playing with twelve cards is laid down in Law 46. Y is liable for any revoke he may have made.

CASE 83.—A and B hold four honors, but score only two. The trump card for the next deal was turned and quitted, when Z says, "We are well out of that, partner, as there were four honors against us." B claims that as he scored honors at once he has now a right to score four, as he merely made a mistake in the number, and scored two instead of four.

Decision.—B can score only two by honors.

CASE 84.—B is scoring ; A and B win the trick, and hold two by honors. A says, " The trick and two." B absently puts his score at one, and another deal is completed. A then notices that B has scored only one, and says, " Our score is three, partner : the trick, and two by honors." " Too late," says Z ; " you cannot score your honors now." " I called them," says A, " so we can score them."

Decision.—Law 7 : " Honors having been called, can be scored at any time during the game (see Case 74).

CASE 85.—A deals, turns up the king of diamonds, and on looking through his hand says, " I don't think it is any use your playing, as I have game in my hand." A, B are at the score of two. Z says to A, " Lay your cards down." A, ignorant of the laws, lays down his cards, which are called by Y and Z ; but A wins the trick and adds one to his score, making it three. Y then deals, and turns up and quits the trump card, and says, " You would have been game if you had counted your honors." A claims that he can count his honors now, as he said he would be game, which meant that he had two by honors.

Decision.—A having failed to name his
honors, and scoring only the trick, it is too
late to count honors when the trump card
of the next deal is turned and quitted.
Both Z and A showed ignorance of the laws
of whist—which is not by any means unusual.

CASE 86.—A deals; Y and Z win three by
cards, and claim two by honors, and score
game. Y commences to deal, and has completed half his deal when A says, "Stop;
you were not two by honors. I held the
knave and my partner the king." This fact
is admitted by Y and Z. Y continues his
deal and misdeals, but claims that as he was
interrupted in his deal he must deal again.

Decision.—It is a misdeal. The adversaries, A and B, established their claim (see
Law 50; see also Case 43).

CASE 87.—A and B win three by cards
and claim two by honors, and score a treble.
Y deals and turns up and quits the trump
card, and while sorting his hand says, "Stop;
you are not two by honors; I held two myself. Mark three, not a treble." A and B
say it is unfortunate, and they are very
sorry, but it is too late now to alter the
score.

Decision.—By Law 11 the erroneous score cannot be corrected after the game is concluded, and the game is concluded when the trump card of the following deal has been turned and quitted. In this case, however, if A and B were convinced they were not two by honors, it would be showing a proper feeling if they scored only three by cards instead of a treble.

CASE 88.—A and B win the trick; Z and Y hold two by honors. Z says to Y, "Score two, partner." B deals, and, having turned up the trump card, says to Y, "How are you two?" "Two by honors," says Y. B says, "By Law 7 to score honors is not sufficient; they must be called. Take down your two."

Decision.—This case is almost the same as Case 74. When Z said to Y, " Score two," he to all intents said score two by honors, and thus drew attention to the fact of claiming honors (see also Case 75). Every whist-player, to prevent argument or controversy, should accustom himself to say "two by honors" or "four by honors" when he holds them. Merely saying, " We win the trick and two ; score three," is really claiming two by honors ; but unreasonable men, who can comprehend only the letter of the law, may argue that, by Rule 7, honors were not named, and therefore cannot be scored.

CASE 89.—Y is a player who, if he hold two honors, claims almost invariably two by honors. Now and then, by the forgetfulness of his adversaries, he succeeds in scoring these honors. Is there no penalty for such a proceeding, and for repeatedly making an incorrect claim?

Decision.—The three other players at the table should remind Y that on several former occasions he has claimed honors when not entitled to them, and if he continues to make these false claims they will decline to play with him either as a partner or an adversary.

CASE 90.—Y, Z are at love; A, B at score of one. Y, Z win three by cards, but have revoked; A, B hold two by honors. A says, "We will score a single." "How can you do that?" asks Y. "We add three to our score for the revoke and our two by honors make us game." Y says, "If you add three to your score it makes you four, and at four you can't count honors."

Decision.—Childish as this objection may appear to some readers, yet it is one that I have repeatedly heard. To show its absurdity, we will suppose that A, B were at the score of one, won three by cards, and held two by honors (tricks count before honors); so A and B would count their three by cards first, making them four; then by Y's argument they could not count their honors because they were four. Of course, A, B can score a single. This is an example of a player remembering only that if *at the commencement* of a game players are at four they cannot count honors.

LEADS

CASE 91.—A leads the two of hearts when it is B, his partner's, turn to lead. Z tells A he has led out of turn. B waits a reasonable time and then leads king of hearts, on which A plays his two. B then leads the four of hearts, on which A plays the ace and wins the trick. "Now." says Z, "lead a club." A deliberately leads a diamond. "I called a club," says Z; "have you no club?" A replies, "I decline to answer that question." Z claims that A must lead a club.

Decision.—By Law 62 Z should have called a lead from B when first he had the lead;

having omitted to do so, the only penalty remaining is to call the exposed card—viz., the two of hearts; but A got rid of this card on his partner's king. Hence, Z, by his ignorance of the laws, lost his claim to any penalty.

CASE 92.—A leads three of diamonds when it is B's turn to lead ; Y plays four of diamonds, B plays ace, and Z plays six of diamonds. "Now," says Y, "I will call a trump from B, as A led out of turn."

Decision.—Too late (see Law 63). When A led out of turn, then only could B be called on to lead a trump.

CASE 93.—A having rendered himself liable to be called on to lead a suit is told to lead a club. He looks through his hand and says, " I have no club," and leads a diamond. Y, B, and Z follow suit. Just as this trick is being gathered, A says, "Stop; I have a club." "Too late," says Z, " you have revoked " (see Law 61). "This trick must stand," says Z, "as all four players have played to it" (see Law 63); "you cannot take back your card now and lead a club. I claim a revoke."

Decision.—This case has been much discussed, and even now I believe there are good players who differ in opinion as to whether or not it is a revoke. By Law 63, "If a player lead out of turn, and the other three have followed him, the trick is complete, and the error cannot be rectified." This law, it is claimed, bears on the above case; but it does not, as A did not lead out of turn; he led a wrong suit, and thereby incurred the penalty for a revoke. Law 61 says, "If when called on to lead one suit he lead another, having in his hand one or more cards of that suit demanded, he incurs the penalty of a revoke." Law 73 says, "A revoke is established if the trick in which it occur be turned and quitted." In the above case the trick was not turned and quitted. To claim that the revoke is established when the three other players have each played a card seems introducing a new and unauthorized law for which there is no authority in the laws. From these considerations I am of opinion it is not a revoke, A being just in time to prevent its being so. A's diamond remains an exposed card, the other players take up their diamonds, and A must lead a club, as at first requested.

CASE 94.—Y deals and turns up the king of diamonds. A holds the ace of diamonds.

8

After four tricks have been won Z says, "What are trumps, partner?" Y, being angry at this inquiry, as it shows want of attention on his partner's part, replies, "Why, I turned up the king of diamonds." It is then Y's lead, and A says, "Lead your highest trump," knowing that he will catch the king with his ace. Y says, "You cannot call on me to lead my highest trump. Law 53 says you can only call on me to play my highest or lowest trump; it says nothing about calling on me to lead it."

Decision.—Law 53 says, "A player naming it (*i.e.*, the trump card) at any time during the play of that hand is liable to have his highest or lowest trump called." A elects to call the highest trump when it is Y's lead, and his claim is correct.

CASE 95.—A holds ace, king, queen of diamonds, spades being trumps, there being only three cards in each hand. He miscounts trumps, and forgets that one trump still remains in. He says, "All three tricks are mine." He then leads ace of diamonds, and without waiting for his partner to play leads the king, then queen. Z says to B, "If you can, win that ace." B has no diamond, but holds the thirteenth trump. Must he trump his partner's ace?

Decision.—Yes (see Law 57). A, by his excited play, probably loses two out of three tricks instead of winning all three, as he would have done had he led his cards calmly.

CASE 96.—A leads when it is B's turn to lead. Y says to B, " Lead a club." " I have not one. Take up your exposed card, partner," says B. "You cannot take it up; it is an exposed card," says Y. " It was," says B, " but it is not so now."

Decision.—Y had the option of calling a lead from B or calling the exposed card. He elected to call the lead, and by Law 66 the penalty 's paid, and A's card led in error can be taken up, as it ceases to be an exposed card.

LOWERED HANDS

The absence of laws relative to lowered hands still remains a blot on the English laws of whist. The Americans have remedied this defect. Thus by Law 20, Section 3, American code, " Every card so held by a player that his partner sees any portion of its face " is liable to be called.

CASE 97.—A holds two cards—the twelfth and best trump (spades) and a losing heart. B holds the thirteenth trump and a losing diamond. A lowers his two cards so that his partner sees them, and says, " They are both ours." He then leads his losing heart, which B trumps, and B leads his losing diamond, which A trumps. Is there no penalty for A's proceeding?

Decision.—By the English code, none whatever. By the American code, A could have been called on to lead his trump, when A and B could have won only one of the two tricks.

CASE 98.—A holds three cards, the king and queen of trumps (spades) and a thirteenth diamond. B has turned the ace of spades, and it is still in his hand; it is A's lead. A lowers his card so that B sees them and says, "They are all ours; it is my lead." He then leads the thirteenth diamond, which B trumps with the ace, and A's king and queen win. Is there no penalty for this?

Decision.—The same reply as for Case 97.

CASE 99.—Y deals. A on looking over his hand finds five trumps, headed by the ten (spades being trumps); six hearts, headed by ace, king, queen; and ace, king of clubs. A lowers his hand so that his partner sees every card and says, "I think we ought to win the game with such a hand as this." B holds ace, king, and a small trump, and at once leads the king, and then takes out three rounds of trumps, Y winning the third round and leaving A with the two remaining trumps. Y leads a diamond, which A trumps. A then leads ace, king, queen, and a small heart. Y wins the fourth heart, but loses every other trick, and A and B win five by cards. On examining the hands it was found that Z had no heart, and Y no club; hence if B had not taken three rounds of trumps A and B would probably not have won more than three by cards. Is there no penalty for B's act?

Decision.—None whatever (see Case 97). It may probably be urged that we should decline to play with any one who lowers his cards so that his partner can see them; but it might also be urged that we should decline to play with any one who revokes or leads out of turn; but for these two offences there is a legal penalty, whereas for lowering the hand there is, by the English code, no penalty. The American Whist League have wisely instituted a penalty.

THE REVOKE

The revoke is a fruitful source of dispute. When it is and when it is not a revoke is often a question. By Law 71 a revoke " is when a player, holding one or more cards of a suit led, plays a card of a different suit." But by Law 73 the revoke is not considered complete unless the trick, in which the erroneous card has been played, is turned and quitted, or the revoking player or his partner, whether in his turn or otherwise, lead or play to the following trick. The following cases give illustrations of the disputes that have occurred in my experience.

CASE 100.—Y leads a small spade, two cards only being in each hand, and diamonds being trumps; B trumps this spade with the eight of diamonds, Z follows suit, and A holds four of diamonds and the four of spades. He knows his partner holds the only other trump besides his own four, and says, " It does not matter what I play, they are both ours." A plays his four of trumps on the twelfth trick, and then throws down his spade. Y and Z claim a revoke, but A said, "It did not matter what I played; both tricks were ours, and the trick was not even turned, and I couldn't lead out of turn, as it was not my lead."

Decision.—Strange as it may appear, this case has more than once occurred in my experience, and A, an old whist-player, even on the next day, argued that it was not a revoke, because the trick was not turned and quitted, and he could not lead again, as it was not his lead ; he merely threw down his card, which was therefore an exposed card, and did not constitute a lead. Of course, by Law 73 A revoked.

CASE 101.—A and B require one trick to win the game. Y leads a spade, diamonds being trumps. A at once puts down the best trump and says, "There is game." He throws his remaining cards on the table and says, "You may call those." Among these cards is a spade, and Y claims a revoke, stating that A's throwing down his cards is an act of play which constitutes a revoke by Law 73.

Decision.—A, on placing the best trump on the table, shows game. He intimates it is game, and his statement must be accepted that he meant this card to show game, not that he was playing to the current trick. If A had waited till it was his turn to play, had then trumped the spade, and had then thrown down his cards, it would have been a revoke. To prevent disputes of this description, if a player has not the patience to wait and play the hand out it is more prudent (when requiring only one trick and holding the best trump) to lay all his cards on the table face upwards, and to say, "Whatever cards you call you cannot prevent the best trump from making, and that wins the game." In the above case it is not a revoke; the best trump was an exposed card only.

CASE 102.—A played a club to a spade and held a spade. His partner asked him if he did not hold a spade. "Spade led," replied A; "oh yes, I have a spade." "Play your lowest spade," said Y. Whereupon A played the three. "Is that your lowest?" remarked A's partner. "No; I have the two," replied A. He then wished to take up the three and play the two; but Y argued that, by Rule 61, A was liable to a penalty for a revoke by playing his three, and his two was liable to be called as he had named it. What is the law in this case?

*Decision.—*The bearing of Law 61 has been much discussed, and an able letter from Cavendish in *The Field*, in 1877, argues the case very fairly and justly. Rule 64 says in no case can a player be compelled to play a card which would oblige him to revoke. If A were not allowed to correct his mistake by playing his two and leaving his three an exposed card, just as he would be allowed to do if he had played a diamond to a heart when he held a heart, he would be compelled to play a card which obliged him to revoke. Again, Rule 73 says the revoke is established when the trick in which it occurs is turned and quitted. In the above case Y claims that the revoke is established immediately A plays the three when he holds the two, the *act* of playing being the establishment of the revoke, instead of the turning and quitting of the trick. Taking the bearing of Laws 64 and 73, it appears that Y cannot be supported by the laws as fairly interpreted. Again, it is a principle in whist law that the penalty should bear some proportion to the offence. That the penalty for a revoke should be claimed for playing a three instead of a two of the same suit without power of correcting this error appears a very severe punishment for a very slight offence, and not just according to whist law.

CASE 103.—A having rendered himself liable to have a suit called is requested to lead a diamond. "I have no diamond," says A, and he leads a heart. The three other players follow suit; but before this trick is turned A says, "Stop; I have a diamond." "Too late; you have revoked," says Z. "No, I am in time to save a revoke," says A.

Decision.—A is in time to save the revoke (see Cases 93 and 102).

CASE 104.—Y leads a diamond, spades being trumps. When it is A's turn to play to this diamond he says, "We want only one trick to win the game, and I hold the thirteenth trump; there it is." And he plays this trump to the trick and throws down his remaining cards. Y claims a revoke, as A holds a diamond.

Decision.—This was undoubtedly an act of play on the part of A, and the fact of throwing down his cards completes the revoke. If A had said, "I hold the thirteenth trump; I do not play it to this trick, but merely expose it; you may now call my remaining cards," he would have protected himself; but playing his trump on the diamond and then throwing down his cards is certainly a revoke. It is curious how often from want of patience players will commit such acts as the above, and will render themselves liable to penalties with disastrous results.

CASE 105.—The score is love all. A and B win two by cards, but have revoked. Y and Z hold two by honors. Z at once says, " I will take three tricks from A and B, and add them to ours; then we are two by cards and two by honors—four." " No," says Y. We consult about the penalty for the revoke. I elect to add three to our score, then count our honors, and score a double. A and B claim that this cannot be done, as Z's election to the penalty must be final.

Decision.—Partners have a right to consult as regards the penalty for a revoke. Z expressed his opinion, with which Y did not agree. Had it been a case of calling a lead, or an exposed card, and Z had made his decision as to the penalty, then Z's decision would have been final ; not so with a revoke.

CASE 106.—A and B win the trick and hold two by honors, but have revoked ; the score is love all. "What shall we do, partner," says Y. "Let them score their trick and two by honors," says Z. "All right," replies Y. "Thank you," said A. "Now," said Z, "we will take your three down, and the game stands love all." "You cannot do that," said A; "you have lost your claim to any penalty by claiming that to which you are not entitled. The revoke penalty must be taken first; you could have taken three of our tricks, or could have added three to your score. If you had taken three of our tricks you would have scored three to our two; but when you have permitted us to score three, it is too late to take a penalty for a revoke; besides, you attempted to inflict an illegal penalty, so our revoke is condoned."

Decision.—A's contention is sound by allowing A and B to score three first before taking the penalty for the revoke. Y and Z have lost their claim, besides having attempted to inflict a penalty to which they were not entitled.

CASE 107.—A and B are at the score of two, Y and Z at one. A and B win the trick, but have revoked. Y and Z hold two by honors. Y and Z agree to add three to

their score for the revoke, then to count
their honors, and claim to score a double.
A and B object, and say, " The penalty for
the revoke must first be taken; you have
elected to add three to your score; tricks
count next, so we add one to our score,
making us three; then you score your honors, and you win a single." Are A and B
correct?

Decision.—Yes; but Y and Z might have
scored a double. If Y and Z had taken
three tricks from A and B, adding these to
their own, they would have been three;
then honors would have made them game
to A and B's two; hence, Y and Z win a
double.

CASE 108.—B leads the king of hearts, Z
plays a small heart, A plays a diamond,
Y plays a heart. "No heart, partner?" asks
B. A looks over his hand and seems deaf
to B's inquiry. B turns and quits the
trick, but again says to A, " Are you certain
you hold no heart?" " Hearts led?" asks
A. "I thought it was a diamond led, and
wondered why you asked if I had a heart;
of course I have." "Too late," says Z,
"the trick is turned and quitted."

Decision.—Not too late (see Law 74).

CASE 109.—B leads a small heart, Z plays a small heart, A plays a diamond, and Y wins the trick, and leads at once before gathering the cards of the last trick. B says, "Stop, don't turn that trick. Have you no heart, partner?" "Yes, I have a heart," says A. A waits to see if Y or Z call his highest or lowest heart; finding they do not do so he plays ace of hearts, wins the trick, and leads his exposed diamond. Y argues that as he has led again, the revoke is complete. B claims that as the trick was not turned or quitted, and that neither he nor his partner had played again, by Law 74 it was not a revoke. Moreover, B claims that Y, having led again when it was not his lead, has rendered himself or his partner whenever it is first the turn of either to lead to have a suit called (Law 63). Y disputes both these claims of B.

Decision.—The fact of Y leading again does not complete the revoke, and as the trick in which A renounced was not turned or quitted A can correct his renounce in error. When Y led it was his lead, as he had won the trick, and he is not bound to assume that A held a heart. Although Y's

proceeding of leading hurriedly was evidently (combined with his subsequent claim) for
the purpose of securing a revoke, yet as the
trick was won by him he had a right to lead
again. Y's heart can be taken up, also the
card he led, and he is liable to no penalty,
as A was the original offender. Y and Z
lost a chance of calling A's lowest heart.
A's diamond is an exposed card.

CASE 110.—A and B play two by honors;
the score is love all. Before half the hand is
played out it is found that Y has revoked.
A says it is no use playing any more: "We
are two by honors, and the revoke gives us a
treble." A throws his cards on the table.
Y and Z claim to play the hand out, and to
call A's cards; they do so, and win three
by cards. "Only a single," says Y. A
claims it is a treble.

Decision.—Y is correct; it is a single
(Law 79).

CASE 111.— A, B play two by honors;
score, love all. Y revokes, but elects to play
the hand out. A, B win three by cards, but
B revokes. What is the best way for A, B
to enact the penalty?

Decision.—There is very little choice;
neither side can win the game. A, B can

take three tricks from Y, Z, and make themselves six by cards and score four. Y, Z can add three to their score and score three. If Y, Z took back the three tricks, the score would be, A, B three, Y, Z love.

CASE 112.—Y revokes, but this is not discovered by A, B till Y's last card has been played. A, B claim the revoke, but Y says, " Nonsense, I didn't revoke." Y at once mixes his tricks with those of the adversary, and says, " There was no revoke." How is this case to be settled ?

Decision. — A, B having claimed the revoke, Y is bound to permit the adversaries to examine his tricks. By Law 77, Y having mixed his cards before they were examined by the adversaries, the revoke is established.

CASE 113.—Y revokes twice in one hand ; score, Y, Z three, A, B love. A, B win two by cards. Can A, B win a treble ?

Decision.—Certainly ; for the first revoke they take three from Y, Z's score, making Y, Z love ; for the second revoke they add three to their score of two, making game and a treble.

CASE 114. — Score, love all ; Y revokes twice in one hand, but wins three by cards. Can A, B score a treble ?

Decision.—Yes ; the penalty for the two revokes is taken first, and Y cannot score his three by cards ; so A, B win game straight off.

CASE 115.—Y revokes, but wins the trick. A, B elect to take three of Y's tricks and add these to their own six tricks, and thus to score three by cards. Y claims that this is a double penalty, as it amounts to six— viz., minus three and plus three. A and B insist their claim is correct.

Decision.—It is surprising how often this objection is raised. Probably this is due to the fact that Law 72, Section 1, is not sufficiently definite. It is there stated : "The penalty for a revoke is at the option of the adversaries, who, at the end of the hand, may either take three tricks from the revoking players, or deduct three points from his score, or add three to their own score." This wording has led to many arguments. It does not positively say that the three tricks taken from the revoking player can be added to the adversaries' tricks ; hence, some players have argued that you might as well take three from the adversaries' score and add three to your own. The two penalties would, however, be very different. For

9

example, the revoking players are at the score of three; the adversaries at love. The revoking players win the trick, and the adversaries elect to take three tricks and add these to their own, and the game stands three to three. If, however, the adversaries could legally take three from *the score* of the revoking players, and add three to their score, the revoking players would be one to three. Cavendish has added a foot-note to this law in the endeavor to prevent this misunderstanding—viz., "And add them to their own." Yet within the past six months I have twice known it disputed that the three tricks taken from the revoking players can be added to the adversary's tricks.

CASE 116.—Y has rendered himself liable to have the highest or lowest of a suit called. A leads a heart, and calls on Y to play his highest heart. Y plays the knave, and B wins the trick. B leads another heart, A plays the ace of hearts, and Y plays the queen. "A revoke," says A; "I called your highest heart and you played the knave, holding the queen." "Nonsense," replies Y, "my knave and queen were of the same value; it didn't in the least matter which I played; it is not a revoke."

Decision.—Y by a want of knowledge of the laws deliberately revoked (Law 61).

CASE 117.—Y has named the turn up trump—viz., king of diamonds. He is called on to play his highest trump; he plays the king, but it is afterwards discovered he holds the ace.

Decision.—Similar to Case 116; it is a revoke.

CASE 118.—Y is shuffling the cards while A is dealing; he drops two cards, and picks these up, as also one of the cards that A has dealt to him, and is unaware of having done so. At the end of the hand Y is a card short, and this card is at length found in the other pack. A and B search the tricks, and find that Y has revoked. Y claims that as the card is in the other pack it is a misdeal, and he is not liable for a revoke. B says, "I believe I saw you take up one of the cards dealt you, and put it in the other pack." "Then," says Y, "it is not a revoke, as you are as much to blame as I am. You ought to have told me I had taken up one of my dealt cards." B states that it is not his business to prevent his adversaries from committing blunders.

Decision.—Y has revoked (Law 46). B is

not bound to tell Y of his blunders, even if
he were certain that Y had put into the
other pack one of the cards dealt to him.
At whist a player must look after his own
and his partner's interest, not the interest of
his adversaries.

CASE 119.—Y deals, and Z wins the first
trick. Y gathers the four cards of this trick
and with it his trump card, and packs the
five cards together. Three rounds of trumps
are then taken. On the third round Y announces he has no trump. Z stops Y from
playing and says, "I know you have a
trump, the turn up trump." Y looks through
his hand, but finds no trump; he then counts
his cards, and finds he is a card short. What
is to be done?

Decision.—The tricks may be counted
face downward, and in the first trick there
would be found a card too many; this
trick may then be searched and the trump,
the extra card, restored to Y's hand (Law
70).

CASE 120.—The same case as above, but
Y on the third round of trumps does not
follow suit; this trick is turned and quitted,
and Z plays again, but says to Y, "I am
sure you must hold a trump." As before,

the tricks are searched and Y's trump is found in the first trick.

Decision.—Y has revoked (Law 70).

CASE 121.—A leads a heart, Y plays a heart, B plays a diamond, Z plays a heart and wins the trick, which is turned and quitted by Y. Z leads another heart, A, Y, and B each play a heart, and Z at once points out that B has revoked, as he played a diamond to the previous lead of hearts. B admits this, and says his sight is bad, and he thought it was a diamond led; this revoke causes the loss of the game. B says, "I beg your pardon, partner; I am very sorry." A replies, "I thought you knew enough about whist to be aware that you must follow suit." B says, "If you treat my mistake in that way, I may tell you that you are nearly as much to blame as I am, as you did not ask me if I. held a heart when you saw me play a diamond to a heart led." A says, "I should have thought it a piece of impertinence on my part to ask if you held a heart when you deliberately played a diamond."

Decision.—A is almost as much to blame as is B for the revoke. Whenever a player does not follow suit, his partner ought to ask him if he is certain he does not hold any of the suit led. Also, if a player is legally called on to play the highest or lowest of a suit, his partner should ask him if the card played *is* in accordance with the penalty. When a suit is called, and a player states he has none of the suit (see Case 103), the player in like manner should ask his partner the question. When a player has made one mistake he not unusually becomes flustered and is very likely to commit another error, and a partner should endeavor to prevent this.

CASE 122.—A and B having won two by cards, and having played four by honors, claim game. Y and Z throw their cards face upward on the table, A and B do the same. Y then notices that A has revoked, and claims the penalty. A contends that as Y and Z have thrown down their cards they have abandoned the game, and therefore cannot claim the revoke.

Decision.—Considering that Law 59 specially decides this case, it is curious how often A's erroneous contention is advanced as an objection to the revoke being claimed.

CASE 123.—A and B are playing against Y and a dummy. A card from dummy's hand is dropped on the floor; its absence is not noticed till the end of the hand. Dummy has revoked. What is the penalty?

Decision.—None; dummy is not liable for a revoke.

SCORING

Scoring by whist markers is merely an aid to the memory.

CASE 124.—A and B score the trick, and claim two by honors and score three. A deals, and wins two by cards and claims game, but Y says, "You were not two by honors in the former hand; I held two honors myself," and he names them. A says it is too late, and disputes that Y held two honors. What is to be done?

Decision.—This comes to a question of facts. A and B scored the trick, and claimed two by honors, and scored these; Y should at once have objected, when the proof that A and B did not hold two by honors would have been easy. If Y can prove that in the former hand he held two honors, it is not too late to correct the score (see Law 11).

CASE 125.—A and B in the first hand win a treble; during the second hand A knocks his scorers off the table. He picks this up, and one of the indicators has been knocked down, showing a double. A and B win another treble, and claim a bumper; but Y disputes this, and claims a treble double is all A and B can score, as only a double is marked.

Decision. — The erroneous *score* of the double having been proved, A and B can score a bumper.

CASE 126.—A and B win a treble and score it. In the next hand A and B win two by cards. In the third hand Y and Z win three by cards and hold two by honors, and claim a double. A, who is scoring, puts down the whole of his score—namely, the treble and the two. In the following hand A and B win three by cards and hold two by honors, and B says, "A treble single and the rub., six points." Y disputes this result, and, pointing to A's score, says, "You are nothing up; how can you be the rubber?" "We won the first treble," says B. "But you have not scored it," says Y. "We claimed and scored it," says B, "but my partner seems to have put it down again." "Then you can't claim it," says Y.

Decision.—If it is a fact that A and B won a treble in the first hand, the marking down of this treble does not prevent A and B from scoring it.

It is essential, in order to prevent disputes, that the scoring should be carefully attended to, as also to prevent loss. As a bystander I once witnessed the following: In the first hand A and B won a treble. In the second hand they won two by cards and held four by honors, but they claimed only two by honors, and scored only as far as four. In the third hand Y and Z won game and marked a single, when A, who was scoring, put down the whole of his markers. In the fourth hand Y and Z won three by cards and held two by honors, and claimed a single and the rubber, three points, which A and B cheerfully paid, instead of receiving eight points, which they would have received had they scored correctly. D, a bystander, who was betting on the rubber with Z, was an interesting study, as he noticed A and B's blunders; but, of course, according to the etiquette of whist, he could not speak.

CASE 127.—A and B win the trick and score it. Y and Z hold two by honors. After A has scored the trick Y says to Z, who is scoring, "Score our two." Z does so.

A deals, and having turned up the trump card, inquires how Y and Z are two. "Two by honors." says Y. "You never named honors," says A, "and by Law 7 to score honors is not sufficient." "To all intents I did name them," says Y, " when, after you had scored the trick, I told Z to score our two. How could we be two except by honors?" "You did not name them, and you cannot score them," says A.

Decision.—See Case 2 in Cavendish, and Case 88 in preceding cases. Y practically claimed his honors.

CASE 128.—A and B win three by cards, and name three by cards, and score three. No objection is made to this score by Z. Y, however, is lighting a cigar during this scoring and until the two packets of tricks are mixed; he then says, "What are you scoring?" "Three by cards," remarks A. "Only two by cards," says Y. Y then takes the pack, and laying it out in fours, says, "You cannot show me how you won three by cards." As some of the cards are mixed, A and B state they are not called upon to prove how they won three by cards. They claim that their score is correct, and that Y

has no right to question the score at this
late period.

Decision.—Y's claim is frivolous and vex-
atious. The time to object was when the
adversaries were scoring three by cards, and
before the two packets were mixed. To
dispute a score after the proof of that score
is very difficult is unjust. It ought to be
made when its proof or disproof exists.

MISCELLANEOUS CASES

CASE 129.—A has dropped the three of
hearts face upwards on the table; it is therefore an exposed card, liable to be called. It
is B's lead, and he leads a thirteenth card,
trumps being all out. A plays his exposed
card, viz., the three of hearts, on this thirteenth card. Y objects, and says, "We won't
have that card now; I have not called it;
you must play some other card, and your
three of hearts must remain an exposed
card."

Decision.—This erroneous contention of
Y's is of frequent occurrence. A player
cannot be prevented from playing his exposed card. A can get rid of his three of
hearts on his partner's thirteenth card. This

is another example of the fact that a player who is ignorant of the laws of whist often attempts to claim penalties to which he is not entitled, and hence renders himself disagreeable as a member of a rubber.

CASE 130.—Two tables, each with four players—viz., A, B, C, D, and W, X, Y, Z—have been formed. After one rubber has been played, A, who is dissatisfied with his partner's play, says, " I have had enough of this." He gets up and proceeds to the second table, touches the table, and says, " I will come into this table." B, C, and D claim that he cannot do so, and that two of them have a prior right to him. A contends that as he first touched the table and announced his intention, he has the right to enter that table.

Decision.—Law 25 is clear: A, having broken up a table, the remaining players have the prior right to him of entry to another table.

CASE 131.—Z is a player who has repeatedly made very rude remarks to whoever has been his partner, such as accusing this partner of trying to lose as many tricks as he could, etc. A, B, C, and D at length decide that they will not play in the same

rubber with Z ; but as Z is usually first in
the whist-room, and claims his right to cut
into the first rubber, the four players who
object to play with him are in doubt as to
what to do.

Suggestion.—Z's greatest friend should be
sought for and informed how the matter
stands, and he should be asked to inform Z
of this. Should Z still persist on his right
to join the rubber, the four players might
tell him they have all agreed that they will
not play in the same rubber with him, and
give their reasons for this decision. Such a
state of affairs is most unpleasant, but not
without precedent. When in India I was
secretary of the whist at a club where whist
was largely played, and for high stakes. An
account of each day's play was kept, and was
made up weekly. On Monday morning this
list was placed in the card-room, showing
the debtor and creditor account. By three
o'clock on Monday each debtor was required
to pay his losses. On the Tuesday following I gave cheques to the winners. I was,
of course, unable to pay the winners unless
the losers paid me first. One member of
the club had on former occasions failed to
pay his losses for a week, and I had weakly

paid the winners from my private purse. To stop this proceeding, I called a meeting of about a dozen of the most influential whist-players, and we agreed that any player who had not paid his losses by 4 P.M. on Monday was to be pronounced a defaulter, and not allowed to play whist till he had paid. At half-past four on Monday this gentleman entered the whist-room and claimed to join a rubber. I pointed out to him the notice that he was a defaulter, and owed 300 rupees for the last week's whist, and could not be permitted to play until he had paid his debts. He promised to send me a cheque on the following morning; on which I told him that when I had received the cheque and it had been cashed, he could play, but not before. As there were some twenty winners who must wait for their money until all losses had been paid, I had a large majority to back me up. As it turned out, this decisive action probably saved this individual from serious loss, as he was a very bad player, and bet recklessly; and as results proved, it was a fortnight before he paid his losses, and then only by the help of a friend.

Unpleasant action has therefore sometimes to be taken even with such a social game as whist ought to be. No doubt remarks are sometimes made at whist which if made on every-day subjects would be considered insulting; but plain-speaking at whist has become conventional, and when this refers to the manner in which the cards have been played, or misplayed, it is, or should partake, of the character of a scientific discussion, where an unsound proof is spoken of as baseless and wrong. It is particularly trying, not only to the patience but to the temper, to have as a partner a man who seems to take great trouble to go out of his way to lose tricks; but it should not be forgotten that this man is certainly doing his best, and it is his misfortune, not his fault, if nature has not given him those intellectual powers necessary to enable him to be a whist-player. That, however, which is the most trying is when this player asserts that he has played every card correctly, that he should play exactly the same again, that his partner is finding fault without cause, and that the partner has played badly. Even these proceedings may be tolerated, unpleasant though they are. It is, however, when a player makes rude, personal, and offensive remarks, too often without cause, that it is time for those other players, who do not desire that there should be a breach of the peace, to decline to play in the same rubber with the offender.

CASE 132.—A leads the king of hearts, spades being trumps; B plays the three of hearts; A then leads the queen of hearts; B plays the two of hearts. A then leads a trump and finds his partner holds only two small trumps. At the end of the hand A says to B, " You surely were not strong enough to ask for trumps with only two small trumps in your hand." " Ask for trumps?" replies B. " I did not ask for trumps. That is just like you, accusing me of offences which I did not commit. It was your bad play in leading trumps that lost us the game, and then you blame me for your own blunders." A then shows the first trick on which B played his three, and the second trick on which B played his two, and says, " You asked for trumps in my first two leads." " That shows how little you know of whist," replies B. " If you read Cavendish you will see that asking for trumps is throwing away, or playing, an unnecessarily *high* card. Now I did not play a high card.

I played the three, a very low card, and as I held the two, it did not matter which I played. I held the eight of hearts, and if I had intended to ask for trumps, I should have played my eight to your king, and then my three to your queen. So, you see, you are quite wrong. You ought to know something more about whist before you find fault with me, as you are always doing, because I know I play a better game than you do, and make fewer blunders."

Suggestion.—Here is a case, which is not merely imaginary, where it is useless to argue or discuss with the player, and where it would be justifiable for other players to decline to play in the same rubber with him, not perhaps on account of his obtuseness and wrong-headedness, but because of the offensive remarks he makes to his partner, when he himself is entirely wrong and his partner right.

CASE 133.—Y, a visitor to a club, enters the whist-room, where there are two tables at which there are four players. At one table shilling points are played, at the other table half-crown points. Y looks on at the half-crown table, and when the rubber is finished, he asks if he may cut in. "Certainly," is the reply. He loses the rubber, which amounts to a treble double, seven points. He places seven shillings on the table for his loss, but the adversary to whom he offers this says, "Seven points—seventeen and six." "I thought you were playing shilling points," says Y. "I should not have joined the rubber had I known it was half-crowns. I never play above shillings." And he makes no sign of paying the extra money. What is to be done?

Decision.—Y must have seen the stakes paid for the rubber at which he was a looker-on. Before joining the rubber he ought to have asked what were the stakes. Having joined the rubber and lost seven points, he must pay up seventeen and six, look pleasant, and be wiser in future.

CASE 134.—Z, a visitor to a club, joins a rubber. Whenever the cards are cut for him to deal he places the pack very rapidly just below the table, and makes with them the noise of rapidly passing his thumb down the side of the pack. He is particularly lucky in turning up an honor. What should be done?

Decision.—The other players should request Z to reunite the pack when cut with one hand only, and intimate that to place the pack below the table was irregular. It might also be desirable to detail some member acquainted with the " pass " to keep watch on Z.

CASE 135.—B wins a trick, gathers this and places it among the other tricks which he has collected ; he leads again, and when it is A's turn to play A says, " I want to see the last trick." Y immediately turns up one of his tricks. A looks at this, and says, " That is not the last trick ; show me the last trick, B." Y at once says, by Law 91, " Under no circumstances can more than eight cards be seen during the play of the hand. You can't see the last trick now."

Decision.—A asked to look at the last trick. Y's act of showing four cards which did not constitute the last trick was a voluntary and gratuitous act on his part, which in no way interfered with A's demand to see the last trick. If the last trick had been won by Y, and A asked to look at the last trick, and B turned up and showed a trick, I am of opinion that A should lose his right to see the last trick. This case often occurs, but is not provided for in the laws.

CASE 136.—Z has rendered himself liable

to have a suit called. A says, "Will you
enact the penalty, partner?" "No," says B,
"I would rather you would." A however
again asks his partner to enact the penalty,
but B refuses, because he considers A is the
better player. Is B's refusal sound?

Decision.—Certainly not. As it is Z who
can be called upon for a lead, B will be last
player, and therefore must derive a greater
advantage than could A from any lead. At
pages 35 and 39, *Art of Practical Whist*, I
pointed out this fact, and showed the advantage of the player on the right of the lead-
er being the one who ought to call the lead.

I am gratified to find that this fact has
been cleverly dealt with, in the "American
Laws of Whist." Law 24 is : "If any player
leads out of turn a suit may be called from
him or his partner the first time it is the
turn of either of them to lead. The penalty can be enforced only by the adversary
on the right of the player from whom a suit
can be lawfully called."

It is satisfactory to find that after a suggestion has been published fourteen years it
is at last adopted in America, although not
in England.

CASE 137.—Y is a player who immediately a trick is turned and quitted asks to look at this trick. He does not do this only once or twice during the rubber, but frequently a dozen times. Can nothing be done to check this annoying proceeding?

Decision.—By the English laws nothing. At pages 39 and 40, *Art of Practical Whist*, I called attention to the abuse of Law 91, by which a player can look at the last trick, and expressed the opinion that Law 91 should be abolished. I am glad to find that by the American laws this has been done. Law 37 is: " When a trick has been turned and quitted, it must not again be seen until after the hand has been played. A violation of this law subjects the offender's side to the same penalty as in case of a lead out of turn."

CASE 138.—Y leads the three of hearts, B plays the queen of hearts, Z the four of hearts. Before playing, A says, " Is that your queen, partner?" "Yes," says B. "Then I will let you win it," says A, and A plays the five of hearts. Y holds the ace of hearts, and claims that A by his remark plainly intimated that he held a card higher than the queen, and that he is liable to some penalty for this. A says, "Show me any law by which I can be punished, and of course I will submit to that law; but there is nothing that refers to it."

Decision.—There is no law, but the " Etiquette of Whist" says, " No intimation whatever, by word or gesture, should be given by a player as to the state of his hand or of the game.

CASE 139.—W and X are two bystanders. W bets with X on the rubber, and W backs A and B. In the third game A and B win three by cards and hold two by honors; they score their three by cards, but forget their honors. As soon as the cards are cut for the next deal W, under the delusion that honors cannot be counted after the cards are cut for the next deal, says, " Why did you forget to count your honors?" A and B then count their honors, and score game and rubber. Y and Z demand that W pays their stakes, which W does on being shown Law 88. X then says, "And you must pay me the bet, too." W objects, and claims the bet from X.

Decision.—Law 88 says: "If a bystander makes any remark which calls the attention of a player or players to an oversight affecting the score, he is liable to be called on, *by the players only*, to pay the stakes and all bets on that game or rubber. X was not a player, and therefore loses his bet to W.

CASE 140.—Z has rendered himself liable to have a suit called, and it has been agreed that B exacts the penalty. B slowly runs through the cards; he then looks at the last trick, and again looks through his cards. Z, losing patience, leads a card (a heart). "Stop," says B; "that is an exposed card; I call a club." Z claims that by Law 87 he is bound to wait a reasonable time only for the decision of his adversaries, and B was a most unreasonable time before he claimed his penalty.

Decision.—What is a reasonable and what an unreasonable time is always open to question, especially if the penalty is not quickly taken. The wording of Law 87 is bad. If it said, "The offender is bound to wait for the decision of his adversaries," the law would be definite. As it stands, it sometimes leads to disputes which cannot well be settled, because "a reasonable time" is vague.

CASE 141.—Z drops a card from his hand; it falls on the table, but not face upwards, yet at such an angle that A sees it. "That is an exposed card," says A; "leave it on the table." "It is not an exposed card," says Z; "it fell face downwards on the table." (See Law 56, Section II.) "It is no matter which way it fell on the table," says A. "It was detached from your hand, and I can name it; it was the king of clubs." A was correct, it was the king of clubs.

Decision.—By Law 60 the card, having been named by A, is an exposed card, and can be called. Here, however, is a contradiction in the laws. Z could not possibly gain an advantage by exposing a card to A only, yet he is punished for so doing by having this card treated as an exposed card.

CASE 142.—Half a hand is played out when Y says, "I can win the rest, it does not matter what you play." A and B claim that Y must lay his cards on the table to be called. Y objects.

Decision.—By the English code there is no penalty for making this remark, though it is a silly thing to say. By the American code (Law 36) Y's partner's cards must be laid upon the table, and are liable to be called. I have grave doubts whether the American law fully meets the case. For example, suppose Y held ace, king, queen, and two small trumps, and the only two remaining trumps were in the hands of A. To compel Y's partner to expose his cards would not help A and B, as Y would lead his ace, king, queen, and thus draw A's trumps. If, however, both Y and his partner were compelled to lay their hands on the table to be called, Y's two small trumps could be called, and A could probably have won both. I have frequently suggested to those players who have a tendency to make unnecessary remarks at whist, the following advice : When you are about to make a remark, think what benefit you can gain by making it, then consider what damage you may suffer. If you find you can gain no advantage, and may incur some penalty, it is wiser not to speak.

Remarks such as those mentioned in the above case are too often made, because a player mistakes holding winning cards for a proof of skill as a whist-player.

CASE 143.—Y and Z are six tricks up, and require only the odd trick to win the game. Z leads a club, B plays a small club, Y hesitates before he plays, when Z, seeing this hesitation, says, "We only want the odd trick, partner." Y then plays the ace of clubs, and wins the game. On examining the cards in Y's hand, it was found that he held ace and queen of clubs, and was really hesitating whether he should finesse his queen. A held the king of clubs single, and had Y finessed the queen, Y and Z would have failed to win the game. A and B claim that Z's remark directed his partner how to play, and that there must be a penalty for such an offence.

Decision.—By the English code there is no *law* to prevent such a remark, nor can a penalty be inflicted. Under the head of Etiquette, " No intimation whatever, by word or gesture, should be given by a player as to the state of his hand or of the game." But this is not a law. By the American code (Law 35), "If any one, prior to his partner's playing, calls attention in any manner to the trick or to the score, the adversary last to play to the trick may require the offender's partner to play his highest or lowest of the suit led, or, if he has none, to trump or not to trump the trick." This law in the American code fully meets the above case, and is a just and reasonable law. The less that is left to etiquette and the more that is defined by law the better.

CASE 144.—Z deals and turns up the king

of clubs. A and B are at the score of four, and therefore require only the odd trick to win the game. When A and B have won five tricks and it is Y's lead, A separates the ace and queen of clubs from his other cards, and shows these to Y, and says, " It does not matter what you play, I must win these two, and that makes us game." "Thank you," says Y ; " those two cards are exposed cards ; you must lay them on the table." Y then leads a small club (trumps), and calls A's queen on his partner's king, and A and B in consequence do not win the odd trick. A argues that Cavendish, under the heading of " Cases and Decisions," writes, " In a perfect code there should be a penalty for all errors and irregularities by which the player committing them or his side *might* profit ; and on the other hand, there should be no penalty for errors by which he who commits them *cannot possibly* gain an advantage." "I could not possibly gain an advantage," says A, " by showing you my ace and queen of trumps, hence there ought to be no penalty." Y replies, " I stand by the laws. Law 60 gives it that your ace and queen of clubs are exposed cards, and I call the queen."

Decision.—Y is correct by the laws. A assumes that he could not possibly have pulled out the wrong card, and have played his queen on the king, yet such things do occur. A also assumes that he could not possibly have dropped his queen face upwards on the table, and have thus made it an exposed card, yet this sometimes takes place also. Cavendish says, " In a perfect code," etc., but the English code is not perfect by any means. A should study the suggestion at the end of decision in Case 142, and try to discover what advantage he could gain by showing his ace and queen of trumps to Y.

CASE 145.—Towards the end of the hand it is Z's lead. Previous to Z leading, A takes a card from his hand, and placing it face downwards on the table, says, " Whatever you lead, I shall play this card." Z leads an unexpected card and calls on A to play the card on the table. A says he cannot be called on to play a card which would cause him to revoke (Law 64). Z says, " You must play that card, but you can correct your error after playing it if it cause you to revoke, and that card becomes an exposed card."

Decision.—Z is correct. A, having stated he will play that card, is equivalent to playing it. He can save the revoke by substituting another card, but the card he placed on the table becomes an exposed card. What advantage A could gain by his proceeding may be a subject for his consideration.

CASE 146.—The cards are cut for A to deal. A proceeds with the deal, but the last card comes to Z. A says, " I cannot understand how I misdealt; I dealt only one card at a time." A then cuts the cards for Y to deal, and Y commences dealing, but after dealing six rounds he deals a card belonging to A's pack, this card having been mixed with Y's pack. "I knew I did not misdeal," says A. "I must deal again. I cannot misdeal with only fifty-one cards." Y states, "It is too late."

Decision.—A's claim is not too late. Y has not completed his deal. Previous to cutting the cards for Y to deal A should have counted his cards; or, to save time, he should have said, "I will cut these cards under protest, and will count my own pack while you are dealing; but do not turn up the trump card till I am certain there are fifty-two cards in my pack."

CASE 147.—It is B's lead. B plays a card,

but at the same instant A plays a card of another suit; both cards touch the table simultaneously. Y and Z claim that A has led out of turn.

Decision.—This is a question of fact. If A played before B, it is a lead out of turn. If the two cards came down exactly at the same instant, A's is an exposed card only. No doubt A intended to lead out of turn, but he may be given the benefit of the doubt.

CASE 148.—Y throws down his cards, saying, " It is no use playing, partner. The game is over; we have lost." B then throws down his cards. Z and A, however, retain their cards, Z urging that the game is not over. What is to be done ?

Decision.—A can call Y's cards; Z can call B's cards.

CASE 149.—Y and Z are playing against A and a dummy; dummy omits to play to a trick, but he plays to the next trick. Y then says, " We will have a new deal." "You can't," says A ; "it is as much your fault as mine that dummy did not play to the previous trick."

Decision.—Y's claim is correct. The laws of dummy are the same as for whist, with the exceptions under Sections 1, 2, and 3, heading "Dummy." (See Law 69.)

CASE 150. — Dummy trumps a winning card of the adversaries. Y feels certain he can now secure a penalty for a revoke, as dummy holds a card of the suit he has trumped, this card being sorted with another suit of the same color. Dummy's partner, A, gathers the cards of this trick, turns and quits it, and is about to lead from dummy's hand when Y says, "A revoke; dummy trumped my suit, and there is one of my suit in his hand." A makes no remark, but continues to play. Y, however, says, "It is no use playing," and throws his cards on the table. A calls Y's cards and wins two by cards, and being at the score of three he claims game. Y says, "You cannot score game; as your dummy revoked, your two tricks did you no good. We add three to our previous score of two, and mark a single." "It is a pity you do not know the laws of the game," says A. "If you had not thrown down your cards I could not have won two by tricks. If you look at Section 2, "Dummy," you will see you cannot claim the penalty from dummy for the revoke."

Decision.—A is correct. (See Section 2, "Dummy.")

CASE 151.— At whist, A is last player. Before playing, A says, "Draw your card, partner." B takes no notice. A, rather angrily, says, "Draw your card, partner." B still takes no notice. A then says, "If my partner refuses to draw his card, I suppose I must win the trick." He does so, and then says, "I never saw such a thing before as a player refusing to draw his card when his partner requests him to do so." B says, "Your request was illegal; you have no right to ask me to draw my card." "Well," says A, "of all the absurd errors I ever heard of, this is the most so. I have every right to ask you to draw your card."

Decision.—B is correct, and probably acted as he did to give A a lesson. By Law 85 A should have demanded the *three* players to draw their cards, instead of asking his partner only to do so.

CASE 152.—A leads when it is B's turn to lead, and A leads a heart. Y says, "Stop; a lead out of turn. I call a club." A, being flustered, immediately leads a club. "It is not your lead, partner, says B, and B leads a winning club, on which A plays the club he had previously led, and proceeds to take up his heart. "Leave that card down," says Y; " it is an exposed card." " Not now ; you have called a lead," says A. " But you led out of turn twice," says Y, "and we have taken the penalty for only one wrong lead. Now, B, lead another club." A disputes the correctness of Y claiming two penalties for his having led out of turn.

Decision.—Y is correct. A led twice out of turn, and there is a penalty for each offence.

CASE 153.—A takes the trump card into his hand before Z has played, and on being asked to show it, says, " I forget it." B wins the first trick, and Y says to B, " Now play your highest trump." B refuses, and says the penalty claimed is illegal.

Decision.—B is right ; the dealer only can be called on to play his highest or lowest trump. (See Law 55.)

CASE 154.—During the play of the hand Z names the trump card. A at once calls on Y to play his lowest trump. Y refuses.

Decision.—Y is correct. Z only can be called on to do so. (See Law 53.)

11

TESTS FOR KNOWLEDGE OF THE LAWS

Any person who believes he is thoroughly acquainted with the laws of whist, and could at once decide what penalty should be claimed for certain breaches of the laws, can test his knowledge by giving decisions to the following cases, and then examining the laws and cases, and see whether his decisions have been correct.

CASE 1.—A and Y bet on the odd trick, A wins three by cards, but revokes. Y elects to take three of A's tricks as the penalty. Who wins the bet on the odd trick? (Law 80 and Cases 2 and 4.)

CASE 2.—A separates a card from his hand, then replaces it. Y says, " I call that card ; it is a court card in hearts." Can Y oblige A to play the card? (Case 6.)

CASE 3.— A separates a card from his hand. Y says, " I call that card ; it is the king of clubs." " I don't hold the king of clubs," says A. What penalty can A inflict on Y or Z. (See Law 60 and Case 7.)

CASE 4.—A leads when B ought to have led. What is the penalty? (See Laws 62 and 63.)

CASE 5.—Y leads a heart ; B plays a dia-

mond, and then says, " Stop ; I have a heart."
What is the penalty? See Law 76.

CASE 6.—Y leads when it is Z's turn to
lead. B says, " Partner, shall we call a suit?"
How about the penalty? See Law 84.

CASE 7. — A deals, and immediately Y
leads. A takes the trump card into his hand.
Before Z plays he asks A to let him see the
trump card. " I forget it," says A. What
penalty can be inflicted on A, and what on
B? See Law 55 and Case 153.

CASE 8.—At the end of a hand A has
three cards, B one, Y and Z two each.
What is done? See Law 44, Section IV.

CASE 9.—A omits to play to a trick, and
this is not discovered till he has played to
the next trick. What can be done? See
Law 69.

CASE 10.—A takes into the hand dealt to
him a card belonging to the other pack.
What can Y and Z do? See Law 42.

CASE 11.—When can a player be called
on to play his highest or lowest of the suit
led? See Laws 76 and 86.

CASE 12.—When can a player be called on
to play the highest or lowest of the suit led,
or to win, or not to win the trick? See
Law 86.

CASE 13.—When can a player be called on to win, or not to win the trick, but cannot be called on to play his highest or lowest card of the suit led? See Law 68.

CASE 14.—A, B, Y, and Z draw cards to decide who are to be partners. A draws a queen, B, Y, and Z each draw a king. B, Y, and Z draw again; B and Y each draw an ace, Z draws a ten. Is any more drawing of cards necessary to decide who are to be partners? State who the partners will be. See Law 19.

CASE 15.—A deals, and as soon as Y has led A takes the trump card into his hand. Z, before playing, says to A, "Show me the trump card." "I forget it," says A. B wins this first trick, and Y then says to B, "Now let us have your best trump." Can Y compel B to lead his best trump? See Law 55 and Case 153.

CASE 16.—Y detached a card from his hand, viz., king of diamonds. A says, "I call that king of hearts." "I have not the king of hearts," says Y. B wins the trick, and Y then calls on B to lead a diamond. Is Y's claim justified? See Law 60.

CASE 17.—During the play of the hand Z names the trump card. A at once calls on

Y to play his best trump. Is Y compelled to play it? See Law 53 and Case 154.

CASE 18.—Z says there is only one offence for which a player can be called on to play his highest or lowest card of the suit led, viz., to save a revoke. Is Z correct? See Laws 76 and 86.

CASE 19.—It is Z's deal; he places the pack for B to cut, and in so doing shows the two of clubs at the bottom of the pack. B says, "Please shuffle again, the two of clubs is at the bottom of the pack. Must Z shuffle again? See Law 32.

CASE 20.—A and B win the trick, and hold two by honors; B is scoring. A says to B, score the trick and two. Z deals, and when the deal is completed, says, "What are you scoring." "The trick and two honors," says A. "You did not mention honors, and by Law 7 to score honors is not sufficient; take down two from your score." Is Z correct? (See Cases 74 and 75.)

CASE 21.—A and B hold two by honors, but neither name nor score these till the next deal has been made a misdeal. Can A and B then count their honors? See Cases 49 and 76.

CASE 22.—A and B are at the score of 4.

They hold two by honors, lose the trick, and revoke. Z and Y take three from the score of A and B, reducing them to one. A and B then claim to score their two by honors, being at the score of one. Can they do so? See Law 4 and Case 77.

CASE 23.—A cuts the cards for Y to deal. Y, before commencing to deal, looks at the trump card. What can A do? See Law 41 and Case 50.

CASE 24.—A, in dealing, deals a card midway between Y and B. Y claims that A must allot this card either to him or to B. What is usually done? See case 51.

CASE 25.—The first deal with a pack of cards shows there are fifty-three cards in it. How is the surplus card most readily discovered, the backs of all the cards being alike? See Case 52.

THE LAWS OF WHIST

(AMERICAN)

(As revised and adopted at the Fourth American Whist Congress, May 22 to 26, 1894.)

THE GAME

1. A game consists of seven points, each trick above six counting one. The value of the game is determined by deducting the loser's score from seven.

FORMING THE TABLE

2. Those first in the room have the preference. If by reason of two or more arriving at the same time more than four assemble, the preference among the last comers is determined by cutting. A lower cut giving the preference over all cutting higher. A complete table consists of six; the four having the preference play. Partners are determined by cutting; the highest two play

against the lowest two; the lowest deals, and has the choice of seats and cards.

3. If two players cut intermediate cards of equal value, they cut again; the lower of the new cut plays with the original lowest.

4. If three players cut cards of equal value, they cut again. If the fourth has cut the highest card, the lowest two of the new cut are partners, and the lowest deals. If the fourth has cut the lowest card, he deals, and the highest two of the new cut are partners.

5. At the end of a game if there are more than four belonging to the table, a sufficient number of the players retire to admit those awaiting their turn to play. In determining which players remain in, those who have played a less number of consecutive games have the preference over all who have played a greater number; between two or more who have played an equal number the preference is determined by cutting, a lower cut giving the preference over all cutting higher.

6. To entitle one to enter a table he must declare his intention to do so before any one of the players has cut for the purpose of commencing a new game or of cutting out.

CUTTING

7. In cutting, the ace is the lowest card.
All must cut from the same pack. If a player exposes more than one card he must cut
again. Drawing cards from the outspread
pack may be resorted to in place of cutting.

SHUFFLING

8. Before every deal the cards must be
shuffled. When two packs are used the
dealer's partner must collect and shuffle
the cards for the ensuing deal and place
them at his right hand. In all cases the
dealer may shuffle last.

9. A pack must not be shuffled during
the play of a hand, nor so as to expose the
face of any card.

CUTTING TO THE DEALER

10. The dealer must present the pack to
his right-hand adversary to be cut; the adversary must take a portion from the top of
the pack and place it towards the dealer;
at least four cards must be left in each packet. The dealer must reunite the packets by

placing the one not removed in cutting upon the other.

11. If, in cutting or in reuniting the separate packets, a card is exposed, the pack must be reshuffled by the dealer and cut again; if there is any confusion of the cards or doubt as to the place where the pack was separated, there must be a new cut.

12. If the dealer reshuffles the pack after it has been properly cut, he loses his deal.

DEALING

13. When the pack has been properly cut and reunited, the dealer must distribute the cards, one at a time, to each player in regular rotation, beginning at his left. The last, which is the trump card, must be turned up before the dealer. At the end of the hand or when the deal is lost, the deal passes to the player next to the dealer on his left, and so on to each in turn.

14. There must be a new deal by the same dealer:

I. If any card except the last is faced in the pack.

II. If, during the deal or during the play of the hand, the pack is proved incorrect or imperfect;

but any prior score made with that pack shall stand.

15. If, during the deal, a card is exposed, the side not in fault may demand a new deal, provided neither of that side has touched a card. If a new deal does not take place, the exposed card is not liable to be called.

16. Any one dealing out of turn or with his adversaries' pack may be stopped before the trump card is turned, after which, the deal is valid and the packs, if changed, so remain.

MISDEALING

17. It is a misdeal:

I. If the dealer omits to have the pack cut and his adversaries discover the error before the trump card is turned and before looking at any of their cards.

II. If he deals a card incorrectly and fails to correct the error before dealing another.

III. If he counts the cards on the table or in the remainder of the pack.

IV. If having a perfect pack he does not deal to each player the proper number of cards and the error is discovered before all have played to the first trick.

V. If he looks at the trump card before the deal
is completed.

VI. If he places the trump card face downward upon his own or any other player's cards.

A misdeal loses the deal unless during
the deal either of the adversaries touches a
card or in any other manner interrupts the
dealer.

THE TRUMP CARD

18. The dealer must leave the trump card
face upward on the table until it is his turn
to play to the first trick.   If it is left on the
table until after the second trick has been
turned and quitted, it is liable to be called.
After it has been lawfully taken up it must
not be named, and any player naming it is
liable to have his highest or his lowest trump
called by either adversary.   A player may,
however, ask what the trump suit is.

IRREGULARITIES IN THE HANDS

19. If at any time after all have played to
the first trick, the pack being perfect, a player is found to have either more or less than
his correct number of cards, and his adversa-

ries have their right number, the latter upon the discovery of such surplus or deficiency may consult, and shall have the choice :

I. To have a new deal ;

II. To have the hand played out, in which case the surplus or missing card or cards are not taken into account.

If either of the adversaries also has more or less than his correct number, there must be a new deal. If any player has a surplus card by reason of an omission to play to a trick, his adversaries can exercise the foregoing privilege only after he has played to the trick following the one in which such omission occurred.

CARDS LIABLE TO BE CALLED

20. The following cards are liable to be called by either adversary :

I. Every card faced upon the table otherwise than in the regular course of play, but not including a card led out of turn.

II. Every card thrown with the one led or played to the current trick. The player must indicate the one led or played.

III. Every card so held by a player that his partner sees any portion of its face.

IV. All the cards in a hand lowered or shown by a player so that his partner sees more than one card of it.

V. Every card named by the player holding it.

21. All cards liable to be called must be placed and left face upward on the table. A player must lead or play them when called, provided he can do so without revoking. The call may be repeated at each trick until the card is played. A player cannot be prevented from leading or playing a card liable to be called; if he can get rid of it in the course of play no penalty remains.

22. If a player leads a card better than any his adversaries hold of the suit, and then leads one or more other cards without waiting for his partner to play, the latter may be called upon by either adversary to take the first trick, and the other cards thus improperly played are liable to be called; it makes no difference whether he plays them one after the other, or throws them all on the table together, after the first card is played, the others are liable to be called.

23. A player having a card liable to be called must not play another until the adversaries have stated whether or not they wish to call the card liable to the penalty. If he plays another card without awaiting the decision of the adversaries such other card also is liable to be called.

LEADING OUT OF TURN

24. If any player leads out of turn, a suit may be called from him or his partner the first time it is the turn of either of them to lead. The penalty can be enforced only by the adversary on the right of the player, from whom a suit can lawfully be called.

If a player so called on to lead a suit has none of it, or if all have played to the false lead, no penalty can be enforced. If all have not played to the trick, the cards erroneously played to such false lead are not liable to be called, and must be taken back.

PLAYING OUT OF TURN

25. If the third hand plays before the second, the fourth hand also may play before the second.

26. If the third hand has not played, and the fourth hand plays before the second, the latter may be called upon by the third hand to play his highest or lowest card of the suit led or, if he has none, to trump or not to trump the trick.

ABANDONED HANDS

27. If all four players throw their cards on the table face upward, no further play of that hand is permitted. The result of the hand as then claimed or admitted is established, provided that, if a revoke is discovered, the revoke penalty attaches.

REVOKING

28. A revoke is a renounce in error not corrected in time. A player renounces in error when, holding one or more cards of the suit led, he plays a card of a different suit.

A renounce in error may be corrected by the player making it before the trick in which it occurs has been turned and quitted, unless either he or his partner, whether in his right turn or otherwise, has led or played

to the following trick, or unless his partner
has asked whether or not he has any of the
suit renounced.

29. If a player corrects his mistake in time
to save a revoke, the card improperly played
by him is liable to be called ; any player or
players, who have played after him, may
withdraw their cards and substitute others ;
the cards so withdrawn are not liable to be
called.

30. The penalty for revoking is the transfer of two tricks from the revoking side to
their adversaries ; it can be enforced for as
many revokes as occur during the hand.
The revoking side cannot win the game in
that hand ; if both sides revoke, neither can
win the game in that hand.

31. The revoking player and his partner
may require the hand in which the revoke
has been made to be played out, and score
all points made by them up to the score of
six.

32. At the end of a hand, the claimants of
a revoke may search all the tricks. If the
cards have been mixed, the claim may be
urged and proved, if possible ; but no proof
is necessary and the revoke is established
if, after it has been claimed, the accused

12

player or his partner mixes the cards before they have been examined to the satisfaction of the adversaries.

33. The revoke can be claimed at any time before the cards have been presented and cut for the following deal, but not thereafter.

MISCELLANEOUS

34. Any one during the play of a trick, and before the cards have been touched for the purpose of gathering them together, may demand that the players draw their cards.

35. If any one, prior to his partner playing, calls attention in any manner to the trick or to the score, the adversary last to play to the trick may require the offender's partner to play his highest or lowest of the suit led or, if he has none, to trump or not to trump the trick.

36. If any player says, " I can win the rest," " The rest are ours," " We have the game," or words to that effect, his partner's cards must be laid upon the table, and are liable to be called.

37. When a trick has been turned and quitted, it must not again be seen until after the hand has been played. A violation of

this law subjects the offender's side to the same penalty as in case of a lead out of turn.

38. If a player is lawfully called upon to play the highest or lowest of a suit, or to trump or not to trump a trick, or to lead a suit, and unnecessarily fails to comply, he is liable to the same penalty as if he had revoked.

39. In all cases where a penalty has been incurred, the offender must await the decision of the adversaries. If either of them, with or without his partner's consent, demands a penalty to which they are entitled, such decision is final. If the wrong adversary demands a penalty, or a wrong penalty is demanded, none can be enforced.

INDEX TO LAWS AND CASES

2

82

Exposed Cards

Laws 56 to 66.   Cases 55 to 65, and 145.

Formation of Table

Laws 16 and 17.   Cases 66 to 69.

Highest or Lowest Card when either can be called

Laws 76 and 86.   Cases 70 to 73, 154, and 155.

Honors Scoring

Laws 6, 7, 11.   Cases 74 to 90, 127, and 128.

Leads

Laws 56 to 70.   Cases 91 to 96, and 152.

Lowered Hands

No Laws.   Cases 97, 98, 99.

Revoke

Laws 71 to 82.   Cases 29, 31, 100 to 123, and 150.

Scoring

Laws 2 to 12.   Cases 124 to 127.

Trump Card

Laws 52 to 55.   Cases 61 to 65, 153, and 154.